Checkpoints and Chances

**Map showing places in Israel–Palestine mentioned in
Katharine von Schubert's reports**

© *Quaker Books 2005*

Checkpoints and Chances

eyewitness accounts
from an observer in Israel–Palestine

Katharine von Schubert

Quaker Books

First published November 2005 by Quaker Books

© Katharine von Schubert 2005
Introduction © Frank Wintle 2005
Appendix © Quaker Peace & Social Witness 2005
Photographs © Katharine von Schubert 2005 except
    p81 and p89 © Jos Koster
Copy editing: Frank Wintle, Seren Wildwood and Peter Daniels

ISBN 0 85245 366 3

Designed and typeset by Andrew Lindesay at the Golden Cockerel Press

Contents

This book is dedicated to those courageous people inadvertently caught up in conflict whose stories appear here.

Prologue

21 October 2002

On Friday, 25 October, I am leaving London to go to the West Bank for three months as a volunteer 'international observer' with the Quakers (the Religious Society of Friends). This project is a response to the call from Israeli and Palestinian peace groups and development organisations to have official monitors on the ground to observe human rights violations and to provide protection to civilians with their presence in the West Bank and Gaza. The UN Security Council tried three times in 2001 and 2002 to establish a monitoring force. Though more than the required nine members of the Council voted positively, America used its power of veto each time to prevent its implementation. Britain also abstained. Yet official observers have been sent to many other conflict zones including Iraq, Yugoslavia and Rwanda.

The Quakers, equating faith with action, have responded, as have several other church organisations in Europe. We are the second team to go out, to support local initiatives for peace on both sides, document the human rights violations we encounter and share in the lives of Palestinians who are trying to exist under occupation. I will be working with a Palestinian community education organisation in Bethlehem, and an Israeli organisation in Jerusalem. I'll be sending emails as regularly as possible. I shall try to write briefly and to the point. In the meantime, thank you very much for your thoughts, prayers and wishes. They are greatly valued.

Katharine von Schubert
Quaker Peace and Social Witness Observer
November 2002 to January 2003
Israel and the Occupied Territories

Further information

Cover photo: Sunrise at Tayasir checkpoint (see report 11).
Photos are by the author, except p.81 and p.89, by Jos Koster.
The original versions of these reports appear on the website of
St Mary's Church, Stoke Newington: **http://www.stmaryn16.org/**
pages/prospect/bullet

Websites with updated information on Israel–Palestine include:
B'tselem, the Israeli Information Center for Human Rights in the
Occupied Territories: **www.btselem.org**
Ecumenical Accompaniers Programme in Israel–Palestine:
www.eappi.org and **www.quaker.org.uk/eappi**
Foundation for Middle East Peace (Washington DC): **www.fmep.org**
Human Rights Watch: **www.hrw.org**
Israeli Committee Against House Demolitions (ICAHD):
www.icahd.org/eng
Israeli Government: **http://london.mfa.gov.il**
Palestinian National Authority: **www.pna.gov.ps**
United Nations Office for the Coordination of Humanitarian Affairs:
www.humanitarianinfo.org/opt

Four observers about to leave for Israel–Palestine after training at Woodbrooke
Quaker Study Centre. From left to right: John Lynes, Katharine von Schubert,
Tony Davies, and Jo Jaffray. Photo: Woodbrooke

Introduction

by Frank Wintle

Herodotus says the word 'history' means 'finding out for yourself'. The dictionary beside me has a close if more clinical etymology: 'learning by enquiry'. Most of us – busy, complacent, indifferent, fearful – are content to let written and broadcast journalism find out history for us while it is being made. Katharine, however, was not.

Sent out originally as a series of emails entitled 'Bullet Points', this series of letters was written when she began a tour as a member of a Quaker Peace and Social Witness team* in the autumn of 2002. She came back to England towards the end of January 2003, and returned later to work for another organisation in Jerusalem, resuming her letter writing in her spare time a few weeks later (with report 18, 'A Bridge too Far').

A peace witness's job is to be where the action is (or, in the case of the stultifying claustrophobia of the curfew, to be where it decidedly is not); to watch, to ask questions, to discover what's going on and to report home, and, wherever possible, to make undesirable things not happen, and desirable things happen. It is Katharine's simple and luminous reportage which arrests us. What does it feel like to be the parent of a suicide bomber? To be a Palestinian suspected of collaboration? To have your home demolished for no sensible reason? To be the mother of small children trapped indoors for days on end in a curfew? Katharine finds out, then tells us in these letters.

❖ ❖ ❖

Growing up in Coventry in the 1970s, a heavily-blitzed and drably-rebuilt city that was fast turning multi-racial and multi-cultural,

---

* The work of this extraordinary project is now under the auspices of the Ecumenical Accompaniment Programme in Palestine and Israel (EAPPI), which involves observers from twelve nations and is administered by the QPSW division of the Religious Society of Friends on behalf of a number of churches (see Appendix).

Katharine as a child was 'fascinated by far away places with sun, blue skies, palm trees, and tribespeople'. She has since rediscovered among the books which influenced her the Barnaby annuals, which have tropical pictures inside, and *Journey to the Source of the Nile*, by Nick Sanders, who cycles from Alexandria to the river's source through Egypt, the Sudan, and Rwanda. 'We – my sister and I – used to play an "Africa" game on the climbing frame, except I thought it was the Orinoco River running underneath (I wasn't very good at geography). All of this filled my imagination, and one day, years later, I had a long talk with my sister about what to study and she suggested Social Anthropology – which I'd never heard of.'

In 1988 Katharine went to St Andrews in Scotland, and graduated in 1992 with a first class M.A. in Arabic Studies, having also studied two years' Social Anthropology and one year's Theology. She moved on in 1993–1994 to the School of Oriental and African Studies at London University, where she read for an M.A. in Area Studies for the Near and Middle East, comprising contemporary politics, Arabic–English–Arabic translation (which would prove vital on location at a tense interview in a cancer ward – see report 17, 'An Israeli–Palestinian Venture'), and Social and Political Dimensions in Modern Arabic Literature.

'When I started at St Andrews I didn't even know where the Middle East was,' she admits. 'So you might say that my path into the Israeli–Palestinian conflict has been rather unexpected. Because I was so interested in African people, tribes and customs, I thought Arabic would be a useful base from which to learn Swahili. However, learning Arabic opened up a new world. The four staff in the Arabic department were all eccentric and brilliant in their own fields, and I caught the bug.' Katharine spent a year after graduation from St Andrews in Egypt, as a volunteer with an emergency aid programme for displaced Sudanese people operating from All Saints Cathedral, Cairo, and later returned for a few years, producing educational video programmes for churches and charities in the Arabic speaking world.

But it was a three-day visit from Egypt to the West Bank in 1991 which triggered a twin passion for enquiry and for justice.

'Those three days taught me more than a year's-worth of history lessons could have done. At that point, I knew nothing of the conflict except what the Palestinian doctors and nurses were telling me, and associated Jerusalem more with my faith as the historic backdrop to the gospels and life of Jesus, than with a political crisis. A flatmate and I took a bus from Cairo to Jerusalem, travelling for twelve hours across the Sinai desert in a convoy of seven buses (for security), escorted by Egyptian police. We had to change buses at Rafah, the border of Gaza and Israel. I recall a Palestinian woman with a child, fellow-passengers, being detained at the border, and not reappearing on the Israeli bus. There was an elderly American couple at one of the visa windows making derogatory remarks about the Palestinians around them, which shocked me. I had never really encountered such blatant discrimination.

'Then on and up by bus into the hills of Jerusalem. On arrival in some Orthodox Jewish area, we found it hard to find a taxi driver to take us to Arab East Jerusalem, to the Christmas Hotel where we were staying. Again, the division and hatred was immediate, in a way that can only shock. I saw brand-new Jewish settlements being built on virgin West Bank land by Palestinian labourers, as this was the only work they could get. And I came to understand, as I was driven through the central street in Ramallah where the stone throwers encountered the occupiers' guns, that the strange term 'Intifada' was a term of resistance (it literally means 'shaking off'). There was fear all around. A people was being oppressed and treated violently. We heard from Palestinian refugees how the Israeli army drove through their camp, invaded their health clinic and terrified the people, and how the Intifada was their way of angrily and staunchly defying this oppression.'

It was another eight years before the emotions kindled by these three days would be put to use. Since 1999 Katharine has worked on projects relating to the Israeli–Palestinian conflict for five British organisations.

❖   ❖   ❖

Katharine's awareness of the Palestinians' plight might lead you to suppose that in what follows she will exhibit an unshakeable bias. But that isn't true. As we were preparing the book she wrote me a reflection on her experiences:

'Gradually an awareness of Israel not just as the oppressor crept into my consciousness. For me, it was difficult to face. But when I was back in Jerusalem I took a Hebrew course, which helped me relate more to Israelis and see what a fascinating and difficult ethnic cocktail Israel is, and how the conflict is affecting everyone in some way. Also I spent more time with Israelis and came to understand their perceptions and how the conflict supported their sense of being oppressed and victimised for two thousand years. The longer I stay around here, the more I realise the utter depth of history and misunderstanding of one side by the other that makes the situation so complex and tragic. Each narrative is credible by itself. But the narratives – one distinctly European and one Middle Eastern, have fatally overlapped.

'I have a strong desire to tell the truths, complex as they can be, because there can be no reconciliation without truth, and without justice. A vast machinery of PR constructed by Israel and its supporters has found a ready marketplace in Europe's guilt for anti-Semitism and the Holocaust, and for the last half a century this has clouded the European and North American mind and hidden a story – the story of one nation growing up at the expense of another. I have tried in my letters to tell that story, which has been largely hidden. Both peoples need safety and a home. But the security of one can never be obtained at the expense of the security of another.'

Katharine's Christian faith, though not explicit in these letters, comes through her writings. 'I strongly believe that faith expresses itself in word and deed. The deed is my natural bent – perhaps because it is easier than contemplation. But I have a contemplative, reflective side, too. It is sad to stand in the Old City of Jerusalem and see the Jews praying fervently by their wall, and the Christians sticking to their rituals and the Muslims on Haram al Sherif, the Temple Mount – all segregated and policed,

*Jews praying at the
Western Wall, Jerusalem*

all divided. Jesus came to look beyond ritual to the heart, to look through the Law and see the spirit of the Law which is love. I feel we in the West are all complicit in the deception that has taken place in this conflict. We have chosen to be blind to the western financial and political involvement fuelling this conflict, which is now threatening global security. That level of complicity and deceit is the thing that bothers me most. We are all tangled up in what is happening and ordinary people are suffering. I hope my letters have opened people's eyes in some way and de-mythologised what is happening.'

❖ ❖ ❖

The last of these reports finds Katharine understandably exhausted, and in a bleak mood. Is this a story of eventual disillusion, of an optimist worn down by the cruel realities of human nature? As a matter of fact, drawing directly from another set of experiences of human nature, I happen to think that it is not.

To begin with, as a proverb goes, 'one small candle may light a thousand others,' and already, through the miraculous samizdat of the World Wide Web, Katharine's letters have been read by thousands of people around the world. I have regularly forwarded them as they arrived in my inbox, and it was, in part, feedback from my contacts which persuaded me to suggest to the Religious Society of Friends that a book should be published.

To get at my second reason to be cheerful, I ought to explain my participation in this project. Twice a year I go for a day to

Friends House, the Quaker offices on the Euston Road in London, to help prospective volunteers on the Ecumenical Accompaniment Programme in Palestine and Israel to prepare for those aspects of witnessing which may involve media contact. The candidates whom I meet in small groups divide neatly into two demographics: those who are fired by their youth, and those whose fire still burns at an older age. The majority, unlike Katharine, are members of the second category, many well past retirement age. One afternoon, sitting with a team which included three of these veterans, and vaguely struck by something half-forgotten that was suggested by one person's knitwear, another's facial hair, and all their footgear, I asked, almost without knowing why: 'Did any of you people go on the Aldermaston marches of the 1950s and early 1960s?' – the marches against the atom bomb.

'Oh yes,' they replied. 'I walked beside Canon Collins,' said a woman, proudly. 'And I was Bertrand Russell's driver, at one demonstration,' said another.

There's a gulf here that intrigues me: I have never met, at Friends House, any individual I could describe as a 1960s or 1970s graduate: those youngsters (and I was one of them) were largely a flashy bunch, interested in the quid pro quo. 'Ban the Bomb' wasn't good enough for us. It had to be 'Make Love, Not War'. The older men and women with whom I work are, of course, those who were children during World War Two, and often its orphans; they meant what they said and did when they were young, they hold the same convictions just as steadily, and they want to write by their actions one last chapter of hope while they still have the time.

I remember that same afternoon, as Katharine and others who were younger looked on with grins, one of the older women put me in my place when I said something like: 'You three, with your grey hairs and aching backs, what can you hope to achieve among millions who are fighting and suffering and hate each other?' Her rebuke was trenchant: 'Isn't it better to do something rather than sit and wail, doing nothing?' Near enough to another proverb, a favourite of my mother's:

'It is better to light one small candle than to curse the dark.'

1. Journey to Hebron

31 October 2002

We left Jerusalem at nine o'clock this morning. Thirty-six kilometres and several checkpoints later, our minibus found the main checkpoint into Hebron city closed off by Israeli soldiers. So our driver sped on. The next turn-off was also blocked – but by three self-appointed guards. Hanging out near their white van in the centre of the side road were a group of Jewish settlers. Two had long dark hair and beards. They all wore dark blue uniforms and had massive guns hanging round their necks. Again, our driver sprinted on along the main road. Then, changing his mind, he turned round, and drove into the side road. The settlers immediately flagged us down and told everyone to get off the bus. To have ignored them could have meant being shot at. So, ten Palestinians and we five foreigners got out, unloading all the luggage which we'd packed tightly into the bus. The settlers separated men from women and told us to stand up against the fence.

Suddenly, my attention was caught as the settler behind us ran out into the middle of the main road, aiming his automatic rifle at a speeding oncoming vehicle which was heading away from Hebron. The car stopped and the settler hassled the Palestinian driver until he got out. Settlers searched his vehicle and took his identity card. As I watched, a Palestinian woman I'd chatted to on the bus came up and put her arm round me. Another settler carrying a gun asked me for my passport. We said they didn't have the right to ask for them or see them. Jewish settlers in the Occupied Territories have no authority whatsoever to control who goes where, except that which they give themselves. The roads do not belong to them. The maze of checkpoints and roadblocks confining over three million Palestinians to tiny enclaves are illegal under international law. What's more, our passports had already been checked by the Israeli army and Israeli police at a previous checkpoint. But our Palestinian driver urged us to show them, so we did and then we were allowed on our way. As it happened, the end of our ride came a few hundred yards further on when the bus

Hebron roadblock

reached an impassable roadblock. So we hauled our stuff out over the mud and walked the rest of the way into Hebron.

Hebron is an ancient Palestinian town. The census figures in 1997 were one hundred and twenty thousand Palestinians. It also has Jewish settlers, in four tiny settlements located in the heart of the old city, numbering no more than fifty families, around four hundred individuals guarded by two thousand Israeli soldiers – that is, five soldiers per settler. Because of this, the city is frequently put under full curfew, as it is tonight, and has been for the last three days. Kiryat Arba settlement on the outskirts of Hebron now houses six thousand settlers.

2. Curfew in Hebron

2 November 2002

We move upstream through hordes of uniformed Palestinian children of all sizes who are coming or going to school (there are two shifts a day – because Hebron has too many school children for too few teachers and buildings). Every shop is shut, every window protected with iron bars. In defiance of curfew, teachers and children persist in going to school, which means negotiating checkpoints. An armoured Israeli police van suddenly drives round the corner. The kids mostly scarper – but there is an opposite movement of a few boys (young teenagers) running furiously towards it to hurl stones. We're in the van's way, so there's no shooting and it heads back the way it came. This is a game of terror.

Up another hill towards the old city, we come to a checkpoint. One of the two soldiers there, a young black Israeli woman, is preventing a group of school girls from going through to reach their homes. It's eleven-thirty in the morning. Bits of words in Arabic and Hebrew fly everywhere. The soldier is getting touchy as the girls try to argue their way through, and a few attempt to get round the checkpoint: their homes are just round the corner. But the two soldiers on duty have orders that 'no Palestinians are allowed through'. 'Why?' we ask. 'These are my orders', she says. She can't give us a reason.

The Christian Peacemaker Team (CPT), with whom we are

Palestinian schoolgirls waiting to be allowed through a checkpoint

spending this week, have had a presence in Hebron since 1995. They are here to reduce violence and, as such, constantly find themselves mediating between the settlers, the Palestinians, the Israeli army and police. Two of us stayed at the checkpoint to see what would happen. After half an hour a boy appeared and was let through. When I asked, 'Why him, and not the girls?' the female soldier said, 'His grandfather is sick,' and then added in an undertone, 'and I know him.' Compassion seems random. Ten minutes later the 'order' changed and all could go through. Fortunate, as it had just begun to rain.

Hebron is a ghost town. Silent market places. Closed doors. Eerie. A tiny boy – about two years old – ran out of an alleyway, with great excitement at seeing us pass by. His brothers had to pull him away. Up near the hospital, away from the town centre, more people ventured out. I asked three elegantly dressed women, 'Aren't you afraid?' 'Afraid of what?' they replied. 'We are only afraid of God.' An old man in traditional Palestinian headdress told us, 'We don't know what the Jews want.'

Curfew means a whole population indoors. People are in a prison here. It doesn't seem a good idea to lock up a whole town on the pretext of security. And the curfews are breeding a terrible insecurity. A few boys approached us, eager to talk. 'This is the third day of curfew this week.' 'What do you do all day long?' I asked. They made a scornful noise. An armoured police van suddenly roared up the street. The boys disappeared but a glass smashed accurately in front of the van as it passed. Even if peace were to come tomorrow, how many years would it take to 'de-program' the violence and hatred out of these young people?

At the border between H1 and H2 – the area where four hundred Jewish settlers live – seventeen Palestinian men were being held by two soldiers. Their coloured identity passes were stacked on a concrete block, and the soldiers were apparently phoning through their identities, to see if any were 'wanted'. Some had been taken in the street at eight that morning, while they were drinking tea. Two more were on their way to hospital. One man had a medicine bottle for his sick boy.

Erez, nineteen years old, holding seventeen Palestinians

I spoke to a paratrooper called Erez, who was nineteen. He was polite (unlike his colleague). He would leave Hebron after another month, and admitted it was a difficult place. One man approached them, signalling that he was desperate for the toilet. He looked in pain. A Palestinian in a suit asked me to ask the soldiers to let him go round the wall to pee. They did. But how embarrassing, and culturally alien, for a foreign woman, free to talk to all and walk through the checkpoint, to see these men being humiliated and incapacitated. Two had been caged off behind barbed wire. We asked for reasons but none were given. It was not until two that afternoon – six hours later – that all the men were released. No reason was given for their detention. They had long missed prayer time at the mosque.

Later – in the evening

It is horrible being so misunderstood. We have just been pelted with stones and rubbish all the way down the long hill into Hebron.

Even though we greeted the people and spoke Arabic, groups of small boys persisted in teasing, taunting and throwing stones at us. I got really whacked on the back. A bag of rubbish was also thrown and caught me and my colleague Bob on the head. This was the manifestation of their frustration at being locked up for four days. We could go where they couldn't. It didn't matter who we were: our crime was being foreign.

To make it worse, thousands of Jewish settlers are arriving tonight in buses for a special Jewish festival: the reading of the story of Abraham in the Abraham 'synagogue'. I highlight the word, as it was originally a fourth-century church built by Constantine, over the cave where Abraham, Isaac and Jacob and their wives are buried. A few hundred years later it became a mosque. After the massacre in 1994 of twenty-nine Palestinian Muslims by the Jewish settler Goldstein, who sprayed the worshippers with bullets, the town was put under curfew for forty days, and part of the mosque made into a synagogue. Tonight, the settlers have the city to themselves. The streets are clear and there is not an 'Arab' in sight.

Next morning

School pupils have just been tear-gassed by Israeli soldiers attempting to break the defiance of Palestinians who are equally determined to keep schools open in spite of the curfew.

3. The Battle of the Hilltops

8 November 2002

It is the most beautiful valley. Tidy terraces dug into the hillsides, silvery olive trees dotted around, vineyards on the valley floor, horses, goats and a powerful scent of gorse. Idyllic rural scene. Driving by on empty Sabbath roads you would not be aware that here, in this valley just north of Hebron, one of the most vicious and destructive battles is taking place.

Atta Jaber is 41, Rudayna his wife, 39, and they have four young children. The Jaber family have owned and farmed much of the valley for centuries. We visited Atta in his third house, and he told us his story. The reason why he's had three is that Israeli soldiers came and demolished his first house because it was 'built without a permit'. On that day in August 1998, the entire extended family – about forty people – stood in front of the house to protect it. The soldiers beat many, including the Jabers' daughter Dalia, who was only two at the time. Twenty-one people were injured. And the house came down. The family were quick to rebuild a second house, much smaller, with only two rooms. A month later, in September 1998, the second house was bulldozed, as was Atta's orchard – a crucial part of his living – to make way for a road for exclusive use by Jewish settlers. When we visited, the entrance road to his house had been freshly bulldozed and a mound of soil and rocks rising to eight feet had been pushed up to make it impossible for any vehicle to pass.

Looking from Atta's house over the settler road to the other side you can see his brother Jawdi's house and a hill beyond. Jawdi

Atta Jaber and his family

owned the hill, and laboured for ten years planting and tending an orchard. In ten hours that orchard, too, was destroyed and the hill has begun to resemble Milton Keynes. Neat rows of red-roofed houses. Settlers have added the hill to their plot, leaving Jawdi with just his house. It is no longer a home at all, really, because the people in this settlement regularly shoot at the house from the hill. [Worse is to come, in report 13.]

This isn't like demolishing houses to make way for a new runway at an airport – this is the systematic destruction and humiliation of a people. Demolishing a house destroys a family. The expansion of Jewish settlements on Palestinian land is feasible largely because of the enormous amounts of funding Israel receives from America, much of which is tax-deductible. What is worse, many Christians who support the expansion of settlements in the West Bank and Gaza, as if to shore up support for a 'greater Israel', are contributing to this destruction. But no one is talking any longer about 'throwing Israel into the sea', are they? The PLO recognised Israel's right to exist as long ago as 1988 (in Algeria) and this was restated at the start of the Oslo peace talks in 1993. Yet throughout the seven years of negotiations the pace of settlement building accelerated – even under the peacemaker Rabin.

Perhaps because Atta's case got publicity abroad, he is now the proud possessor of a document from the Israeli authorities stating that his third house is safe from being bulldozed. He has lost much of his land, however, and his family and home continue to be terrorised by some of the settlers. Yet to a foreign Jewish visitor last month who apologised for what the state of Israel had done to him and his family, Atta said with typical pride and resilience, 'I welcome any Israeli into my house.' He means it.

I'm told that the majority of Jewish settlers in the West Bank are there for economic gains, rather than ideological reasons. They are enticed by the government into cheap housing and subsidised living to occupy some of the most contentious locations in the West Bank. It is a way of making the occupation extremely difficult, if not impossible, to reverse.

Atta's land has been taken from him in the name of security.

This is what Prime Minister Ariel Sharon said in April 2001, according to the Israeli newspaper *Haaretz*:

> *You know, it's not by accident that the settlements are located where they are . . . come what may we have to hold the western security area . . . and the eastern security area along the Jordan River and the roads linking the two. And Jerusalem of course. And the hill aquifer.*

4. Bethlehem Views

12 November 2002

My flat is in a valley on one edge of Bethlehem, looking towards the neighbouring Palestinian town of Beit Sahur (the biblical shepherds' fields). Just over the hill you can see Har Homa, a brand new Jewish settlement which is being built to house thirty

Har Homa, with Katharine's block of flats (right)

Palestinian autonomous areas and Israeli settlements, January 2002

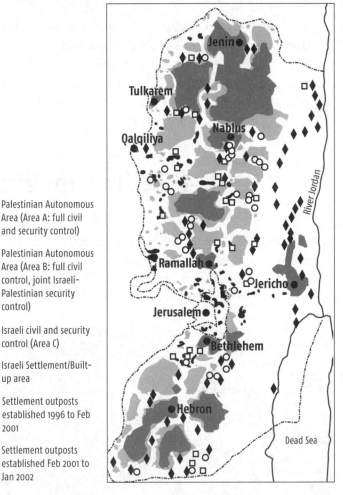

Legend:

- Palestinian Autonomous Area (Area A: full civil and security control)
- Palestinian Autonomous Area (Area B: full civil control, joint Israeli–Palestinian security control)
- Israeli civil and security control (Area C)
- Israeli Settlement/Built-up area
- Settlement outposts established 1996 to Feb 2001
- Settlement outposts established Feb 2001 to Jan 2002

The Oslo Accords, signed in 1993, were an agreement between Israel and the Palestine Liberation Organisation intended to secure peace by, inter alia, inaugurating the Palestinian National Authority, handing over some land to the Palestinian National Authority, and allowing the PNA its own security forces. They were supposed to be the start of a continuing peace process which then stalled badly at talks in the US in the summer of 2000, a failure that was at least a partial cause of the latest Intifada.

Based on a map from the Foundation for Middle East Peace, © Jan de Jong, adaptation © Quaker Books.

thousand Israeli Jews. Har Homa was until recently a tree-filled hill called by the Arabic name, Abu Ghuneim. However, it was confiscated by the Israeli government, and though the matter was disputed twice at the UN Security Council in 1997 by Palestinians upset at the building plans, the US vetoed opposition both times. A new Israeli bypass road is being built to Har Homa that will surround and then cut right through Beit Sahur, where Palestinian Christians and Muslims live peacefully side by side.

Last month (October 2002), Israeli courts upheld an Israeli Army order to demolish a hundred and twenty newly-built Palestinian homes in Beit Sahur. According to the Oslo Agreement, the area where these homes are is known as 'Area B'. This means Israel is in control of external security whilst the Palestinian Authority controls internal affairs including land use. The Arab Orthodox Housing Project received permits from the municipality to build, and was on the verge of completing the project when Israel sent its demolition order. Suddenly Israel claimed the land is in another location called 'Area C' and therefore completely under Israeli control. The residents have demonstrated against the order and launched an international campaign to save their homes. I am spending some days working in Jerusalem with the Israeli Committee Against House Demolitions, run, as the name suggests, by Israelis.

Last week, I heard the mayor of Bethlehem, Hanna Nasir, say, 'Here we are surrounded by settlements. They are grabbing the land around the clock and taking eighty-one per cent of our water. Oppression to this extent doesn't help the cause of peace.'

The settlements are built on each hilltop around Bethlehem and are thus acting to block Bethlehem off from Arab East Jerusalem. Israel occupied East Jerusalem in 1967 and annexed it in 1980, claiming it as part of an undivided capital. The Palestine National Authority, however, wants East Jerusalem to be the capital of an independent Palestinian state. This makes Har Homa a very controversial settlement.

Meanwhile I've met Mary, who is suffering. She's twenty-five and from a middle-class Christian family. She told me her father used to be rich, cutting Hebron stone for building use. Now the logistics of transporting the stone thirty-six kilometres through checkpoints and roadblocks with the necessary permits required, and the risks attached to travelling on settler roads, mean his business isn't viable any more. Mary used to have a nightlife, and was able to get out to Jerusalem or Ramallah to meet her friends. But for two years she's been stuck in Bethlehem, unable to get a permit to leave. She used to be the PR manager of a tourist group in Beit Sahur, but the business folded and now she teaches English in Bethlehem. A lower salary helps to keep the family afloat, although obviously it leaves much less for socialising. She's seriously thinking about emigration as the stress is getting too much. If she goes, she will be one of over three thousand Bethlehemites who have left the town in the last two years, fleeing a dire economy and the trauma of being unable to move around freely.

I just asked the shopkeeper at the top of this hill if he stocked the kind of cheese you put inside *katayif* – this is a special small pancake they sell during the month of Ramadan. His old father, an enthusiastic cultivator, went off to get some peppers for me from his garden at the back. His son, the shopkeeper – Majid – explained that during the Israeli military incursions earlier this year, the only thing the family could do was cultivate their garden. It turns out that Majid runs the local Amnesty International group from his shop. He lost his post as a teacher of electronic engineering during the Intifada. Students who came from far and wide before to study in Bethlehem could no longer get to the classes because of roadblocks and checkpoints, so he's another person whose job has vanished.

By the shop door there was a computer. The hard disk had its top off and wires were visible, but Majid was still able to show me pictures of his shop surrounded by Israeli tanks. He manages the Amnesty group from this old PC. The only reason it functions is because he knows how to fix it when it goes wrong, which is roughly every half an hour.

Walid, meanwhile, is a student at Birzeit University. He doesn't know where he stands politically any more. Though he can no longer meet them, Walid is still in touch with left-wing Israeli groups and refuseniks whom he met at a conference in Portugal a while ago. The latter include the five hundred Israeli reservists who stated in January 2002, 'We shall not continue to fight beyond the 1967 borders in order to dominate, expel, starve and humiliate an entire people.' Another man I meet, Mahmoud, is bored, and spends a lot of time hanging out at the Arab Educational Institute in Bethlehem, where I am also helping out. He told me that he was depressed about prospects for peace, as the numbers of Israelis countering the actions of their government are so small.

A herd of sheep and goats has just passed by my window. If it were not for the stories of the people of Bethlehem, I might not be aware from my home of the difficult times this country is passing through.

5. Olive Picking

18 November 2002

Today I picked olives. The valley, deep in the northern part of the West Bank, was hot and sunny – more than is apparently usual for November. Plastic sheets caught the fruit, as the men whacked the branches with a stick and the women gathered at the bottom. A small group of 'internationals' and Israelis, including a member of Rabbis for Human Rights, had been called out by Palestinians to help them harvest the last of this year's olives from their land.

Not long after we started picking, we saw three settlers on the horizon. Some of the Palestinians froze instantly. Jewish settlers in many parts of the West Bank have a track record of violence towards Palestinians picking their crops and will do anything to stop them. Last Thursday, settlers threw a rock at an Israeli man who was helping the Palestinians pick olives. He ended up in hospital needing stitches to his head.

The land we are picking on is disputed. According to one of the Palestinians, some of the land was registered in the name of

Olive picking   _Confrontation with the Lieutenant Commander_

his grandfather, who died over fifty years ago. There are twenty Palestinian owners for this tract of land, who all live in the nearby villages, but the deeds are locked away in the records office at Nablus, which is under curfew. Just over the hill there is a Jewish settlement (Giliad) which also claims the land. The settlers argue that the settlement was built on Jewish-owned land. They say that some Palestinians sold the land to the Jews.

Now an army jeep appears. After much discussion between army and settlers, some of the soldiers approach. A soldier produces a two-week-old order issued by their Brigade Commander stating that the area is a 'closed military zone . . . except for those I have given permission to be here'. The order is valid for three weeks. We're told we can't pick any more. The Rabbi reads the order and says that the Commander's exception applies to the olive pickers. The soldier admits that he doesn't know enough about the order and goes to consult someone else.

Meanwhile, Israeli police turn up. One starts videoing the group of us, then he suddenly grabs one of the Palestinians and demands his ID, which he hasn't got with him, because he was frightened he might lose such a precious document; so his brother goes back to the village to fetch it. The Palestinian boy is interrogated about the identity of his family, and the police and army then take a long time phoning through the details to someone, somewhere. Our passports are also taken.

Finally a Lieutenant Commander arrives with more soldiers. One tells me that the land is being disputed between Palestinians from two different villages. Another says that the dispute is between the settlement and the Palestinians, and if the Palestinians could produce a title deed from before 1967, when the West Bank was part of Jordan, that would be conclusive on their side. I remind myself that, according to international law, all of the West Bank has been illegally occupied by Israel since 1967, and that the Fourth Geneva Convention prohibits building on occupied territory (see Appendix).

When the Lieutenant Commander steps in, rather full of machismo, the negotiation stops. He tells the Palestinians that this isn't their land and implies in a threatening manner that they should disappear. Fortunately their donkey had already taken a massive sack of olives away. The police were heard saying to the soldiers in Hebrew that they could end this argument very quickly if they chose (i.e. tear gas). In fact, the army is restricting access to two kilometres of land around the disputed area and we never managed to ascertain whether these olive trees were actually a bit of the supposedly disputed part or not.

We left with many of the trees untouched. And as we went, the army spoke through a loudspeaker to other Palestinians they had spotted among the olive groves, ordering them to go away immediately. Once back round the hill, we met some men who had come miles on foot across the hills from Nablus to reach family members in a nearby village. Walking over rough terrain for hours at a time is now the only way that many West Bank Palestinians manage to continue their lives. Under the Oslo agreements vast tracts of land are designated as 'Area C', which is under Israeli military control. The West Bank land controlled by Yasser Arafat's Palestinian National Authority (PNA) is intersected by a hundred and forty-four Israeli civilian and military installations. This makes it virtually impossible for the PNA to control, and renders any so-called 'Palestinian State' non-viable as the land has become a fragmented mosaic of disconnected islands. A fact-finding committee led by former US Senator George Mitchell on 21 May 2001 called on the Palestinian Authority to 'make a one hundred per cent effort to prevent terrorist operations and to punish perpetrators'. It also recommended that the Israeli government freeze all settlement activity, including the natural growth of existing settlements. To date this has not happened.

We were grateful to the settlers for keeping their distance, but sorry that the army found excuses for us not to continue to pick the Palestinians' olives. Army and settlers all work in the name of the state of Israel. The saddest thing I heard was the contempt they both had for the Palestinians, implying amongst other things that we might find they had stolen the cars we came in.

Yet, an hour later, we were all sitting in the house of one of the Palestinian landowners, being treated to honeycomb, mint tea and coffee and many thankyous for coming. 'If you had not been here, they would have beaten us,' said our host before escorting us a few miles across dusty tracks back to the main road. This kind of hospitality and gratefulness is beyond the comprehension of the soldiers we encountered. It would ruin the myth that they are defending 'their' land from Arab terrorists.

6. The Way Violence Works

24 November 2002

There was a swift Israeli reaction to the murders by armed Palestinians of twelve Israeli military and security officers in Hebron a week ago last Friday (16 November 2002). This house was demolished a few hours after the ambush because gunmen were reportedly seen shooting from the roof. Some things are hard to prove: the initial and widely broadcast story of it being 'a massacre of worshippers' was untrue. Though attractive in its simplistic polarisation of 'Palestinian terrorists' shooting 'innocent Jewish worshippers', the story was demythologised when Tzvi Katzover, the leader of the settlement of Kiryat Arba admitted that the shooting started fifteen minutes after the last of the Jews who had worshipped in the synagogue (the Tomb of the Patriarchs) were back inside the settlement.

It was a horrible loss of life. But the gun battle was between armed Israeli soldiers, armed guards from the settlement and armed Palestinians. Military officials have now confirmed that no unarmed Israeli civilian was shot or wounded. Most of the fatalities (four Israeli soldiers, five Israeli border patrolmen, three armed Israeli settlement security guards and three armed Palestinians) occurred when waves of backup soldiers and security officials ran or drove into the dark, unlit lanes between Palestinian homes in the direction of gunfire.

Hebron: demolished house

As usual, knowing the context of the incident is important when you try to understand – not excuse – the reason for the battle. Hebron, under the Oslo Accords, is an autonomous Palestinian area ('Area A') in the West Bank. Yet four hundred armed Jewish settlers who live in the heart of the city hold hostage (in all but name) the Palestinian population of around a hundred and thirty thousand. Two thousand Israeli soldiers protect the settlers and curfews are regularly enforced on the Palestinians, particularly on Fridays, when the Shabbat (Sabbath) begins and settlers including those from Kiryat Arba on the edge of Hebron come to pray.

In a chain reaction, a brand new Jewish settlement has begun to take seed in Hebron this week. I saw young Israeli settler girls camping in tents on the newly bulldozed ground near the centre of the old town, guarded by security and Israeli soldiers. The tents, I am told, will be continuously occupied until they are turned into permanent buildings. Meanwhile, the Palestinian families whose houses are simply 'in the way' of this settlement are facing increasing harassment. I saw the kitchen extension of one house being demolished this Thursday, just as the Ramadan fast was breaking. And I could not repeat the language which the settlers literally spat at us, when they discovered that we 'internationals' were staying overnight with Palestinian families.

Less than a week later (Thursday, 21 November) a Palestinian suicide bomber in Jerusalem killed eleven Israeli civilians and injured more than forty, the first fatal attack in Jerusalem since 31 July. More families had their houses demolished, on the presumption of association with suspected militants. Bethlehem is a 'closed military zone' and has been under curfew since Friday morning. Today I climbed up to the top of one of the hills near my flat to see if the shop was open. As I stopped to catch my breath, I heard, 'Katrin . . . Katrin . . . over here! Come and drink coffee.' So I went, and my quick shopping trip for milk turned into a four-hour visit (including lunch) with this Christian Palestinian family. I had met Rachel, in the shop, briefly, three weeks ago. Today I met three of her four children, her husband, and a neighbour. Everyone is at home, because there is no school, and no work and no shopping.

This is life under curfew. Rachel's nine-year-old daughter was bored and constantly interrupting other conversations. She frantically raced about the house, and showed me her pet rabbits and toys, and then sat watching a video. The family have a green card for the USA, and are seriously considering emigrating. Their older son is already studying there. Work has stopped on the house they were building because – short of selling more of their land – without work, there is no money to spare. Rachel said the curfew was driving her mad. It was just a monotonous loop of sleeping, getting up, eating, and trying to cope with the children. Everyone here dreads a recurrence of the forty-day-long curfew Bethlehem suffered earlier this year.

Curfews punish the entire population, and while it's easy to sympathise with the Israelis' fear of being attacked (I am certainly more afraid in West Jerusalem than in Bethlehem) to enforce a curfew in an already illegally occupied area is no less an evil. Uri Avnery, a former Knesset member, said: 'The first and worst violence is the occupation,' and 'Human rights are not a special favour granted to Palestinians if they behave like good children.'

Hamas, who claimed responsibility for the suicide bomb, said in a statement that it was in response to the Israeli occupation of the Palestinian territories and the killing of Palestinians. Two days before this attack, six Palestinians, including a teenager, had been shot dead in an Israeli raid in Tulkarem, another West Bank city – an incident much less reported. People here are sick and tired of the killing. A Druze lady I met on the bus to Jerusalem the same morning as the suicide bombing felt the futility of the violence: 'This is terrible. It doesn't help them or us. That someone should grow up and do this thing. It's not right.' Ironically, the curfew in Bethlehem, imposed last Friday as a result of the suicide bombing, meant that a non-violent rally in Duha, near Bethlehem, which was being organised by local Palestinian peace groups, had to be cancelled.

Palestinians cannot militarily defeat the Israelis, but the Israelis cannot politically defeat the Palestinians. The Palestinians are here to stay – albeit on the tiny bits of land which currently remain theirs. They cannot be 'transferred' (which several Israeli politicians have been advocating for some time). The anger and bitterness which spurs the violence is palpable everywhere I've been in the Occupied Territories, but so is the resilience and the kindness of the Palestinians I know. I came away from the house on the hill loaded with food in spite of my protests and in spite of the inaccessibility of food because of the curfew.

I sat with an Israeli friend in a café in West Jerusalem this week. She feels at the moment that separation of the populations is the only option. Perhaps it is for now, but it can surely only be an interim solution, before a way is found for Palestinians and Israelis to live together.

7. Conversations with the Family of a Suicide Bomber

27 November 2002

'I didn't know anything about it,' Ayat's father told me today. He smiled sadly. 'Ayat – *Allah yirhamha* [God have mercy on her] – put her secret here, in her heart,' he said, pointing to his chest.

On 29 March 2002, Ayat al-Akhras, an eighteen-year-old Palestinian girl, blew herself up in front of a supermarket in Jerusalem, killing herself and a seventeen-year-old Israeli girl, Rachel Levy. Ayat was one of eleven children, seven girls and four boys. Today I sat with her family for several hours in Deheishe refugee camp in Bethlehem. Their house now has a demolition order on it. It's a solid building, three storeys high and not very far into the refugee camp. The room we sat in was empty of furniture, except for some mats to sit on and a small electric heater, around which the children crowded to keep warm. All their things have been moved into a neighbour's house in case the demolition is sudden. With the help of a local human rights organisation and an Israeli lawyer, they have taken their case to the Supreme Court of Israel

Ayat's father with two grandchildren, fourth generation refugees

and are awaiting the court's decision in the next few weeks. It is not beyond the Israeli army to go above the law and demolish the property first for 'military reasons'. Over the past weeks Deheishe has been the scene of regular house-to-house searches for militants. In actual fact, many Palestinians are arrested simply because they are relatives of other Palestinians on a 'wanted' list. Yesterday Samir, one of Ayat's brothers, was arrested for at least the second time. He was questioned and released this morning. A second brother was taken just after Ayat committed suicide and has been in prison for the last seven months.

'A man would rather be killed a hundred times, than his son or daughter be injured,' Ayat's father told me. 'Thank God, there is goodness in the world . . .' He lost his job the day Ayat and Rachel died. He was working for an Israeli company in Jerusalem. For eleven years he'd broken bread and drunk with Israeli colleagues and sometimes stayed with them. Now they are afraid to keep in contact with him. I asked him if he thought Ayat had considered the effect of her actions on her family. He laughed and described Ayat with great compassion. 'She was very clever. She got ninety-two point eight per cent in the first part of her *tawjihi* (end-of-school exams). She wanted to be a journalist. She was kind; she had a lovely personality. She was engaged ... No, she didn't think of her family.' What did he feel about what she had done? He said: 'To every action there is a reaction' and began to describe the circumstances which he felt must have spurred her to die for the nationalist cause.

Ayat and her siblings are third generation refugees. Her grandparents fled from their village, Qatra in Palestine, in the war of 1948. Qatra is one of more than four hundred unrecognised villages in Israel and has been replaced by the Jewish settlement of Gedera. Ayat's father was born – literally – on the street as his parents fled to Gaza that year. They came out of Gaza in 1967 and went to live in Deheishe refugee camp, which is made up of people from many Palestinian villages around Jerusalem and Bethlehem, all now destroyed.

Life in the refugee camps has been full of misery since the second Intifada broke out. Many children have been shot in the streets of the camps. Over the past couple of years closures imposed on the West Bank by the Israeli authorities, on security grounds, have hit residents hard since by and large they need to work inside Israel if they're to make any money. So unemployment has risen and social and economic conditions in the camps have deteriorated. Peter Hansen, Commissioner-General of the UN Relief and Works Agency for Palestine Refugees (UNRWA) said in a report issued on 7 November, 'Few places have ever undergone as steep and rapid a decline in income and living standards, and as rapid an increase in mass deprivation, as the Palestinian population has been experiencing for the past two years.'

One of Ayat's brothers had been beaten badly by soldiers, and several relatives were killed in Gaza this year. Earlier in the year, Deheishe camp was the scene of fierce fighting when Bethlehem suffered five incursions. Strict curfews remain in force this week, and many inhabitants have been rounded up, blindfolded, stripped and beaten.

Two and half weeks before Ayat died, a neighbour (aged twenty-one) was sitting in his bathroom when he was shot through the window by a soldier. Ayat's brother and cousin tried to carry him to hospital but he died in their arms. Ayat was distraught. I understand this was perhaps the decisive factor that propelled Ayat into the Al Aqsa Martyrs Brigade. Yet no one, not even her fiancé, knew of her intentions before she died.

'Believe me, we don't hate anyone. We want everyone to be happy. We don't like seeing anyone cry,' said her father. 'We hope one day the sun will come out and there will be freedom.' At one point in our conversation, another of his daughters got fed up with the reasonableness and kindness with which he spoke about all people. 'Dad, shut up. We are the victims all over the world.' I guess she was showing sparks of the same anger that had been kindled in her sister. But her father continued to tell me that Islam teaches people to respect those of all religions, and that essentially every human being is the same.

I would like also to meet with Rachel Levy's family to get a sense of their history and to hear a story which must be no less tragic. A journalist friend of Ayat's family did help the Israeli and Palestinian families to exchange phone numbers. I asked Ayat's father if they had called each other. There was good intention on both sides, he said, but the grief of both families was too much to bear. So there has been no contact between them.

8. Death Under Curfew

1 December 2002

What do you do if you go into labour and you can't get to hospital? How do you keep your children entertained all day long in the house? How do you make your bread last? How do you obtain cash, so that if the shops do open you can buy food? What do you do if a family member becomes sick? How do you take your dog for a walk? At what point do you call an ambulance and risk being

Manger Square during curfew

stopped or shot at because of Israeli fears that you may be part of a terrorist plot?

The curfew was expected in Bethlehem as soon as it was known that the suicide bomber in last week's horrific bus bombing in Jerusalem was from the Bethlehem area. People were immediately out in the shops and streets stockpiling food. They knew they could be in for a long haul. And they were right: today is the tenth day of curfew and no one knows if it will be lifted for the *Eid* (end of Ramadan) celebration in a few days' time, or whether it will last until or beyond Christmas.

Yesterday I saw a one-week-old Christian Palestinian girl sleeping in her cot. She was born at the Holy Family hospital in Bethlehem by caesarean section two days into the curfew. Her mother could not stay in overnight, so for three days she went back and forth in a car, breaking the curfew.

Keeping your enemy in the dark is all part of the plot. Last Thursday – the seventh day of house confinement – the Israeli army used local TV stations to announce that they would lift the curfew in Bethlehem for a few hours to allow shops to open, but not until they had changed their minds a few times the night before and during the morning. Get people to hope, then retract your promise. Psychological warfare is important here. Confuse over eighty thousand people – are they allowed out or not? – create fear, then let them out to breathe for just a few hours, before you clamp down on them again.

In my few hours of freedom between half past one and five in the afternoon, I went to Manger Square and into the Church of the Nativity. The tanks that were there last week had withdrawn. The church was almost empty. An old Muslim lady attended to the candles. Then the bell began tolling. After a few minutes voices could be heard chanting and I thought I was in for a treat. But a string of Bethlehemites – men, women and children – entered carrying a coffin. They had had to wait until the curfew was lifted to be able to bury some unhappy member of their family. Out in the town, the narrow streets were tightly packed with people meeting up and shopping, shopping, shopping before the 'lock-up' hour came again. Going home, I felt like Cinderella . . . that the ball had been a dream, 'pumpkin' time was drawing near and the whole town which had been so alive and noisy was disappearing back into silence.

That 'dream', of course, is a nightmare for many Palestinians throughout the towns and villages of the West Bank and Gaza. Many people have been shot and killed because they didn't know the curfew had begun again. A few days ago, a man from one of the villages just outside Bethlehem was shot dead in his car at a checkpoint coming into Beit Sahur. He was thought to be unconnected politically and died – apparently – because he didn't slow down when told to.

A woman whose family I visited yesterday told me that there weren't any fresh vegetables when she went out during the brief respite. There had been no transport for the produce which should have come from Nablus or Ramallah, because both these places are also under curfew. Two people told me independently that their backs ached because they'd been confined to their houses for so long, unable to move. These are long, dreary days for the

Muslims in Bethlehem, who are in their final Ramadan week of fasting all day long.

Bethlehem is in a pitiable state. The five military incursions it has suffered already this year (the current one being the sixth) have meant not only a reduction in tourist numbers from one million a year to a handful but also about £3 million worth of damage to its infrastructure. All natural life has seeped out of it and many families have been reduced to poverty.

Fifty-five years ago this week, the UN General Assembly voted to partition what was British Mandate Palestine into a Jewish state and an Arab state (UNGA Resolution 181/1947). Today, Israel has effectively retaken direct military control of all of the West Bank and Gaza Strip, and the parts which had become independent Palestinian areas under the Oslo Agreements (Bethlehem included) no longer exist.

The resulting facts are staggering: since September 2002 some quarter of a million children have been unable to reach their schools, according to UNICEF. Sixty to eighty per cent of the population live on less than US $2 a day, and movement is virtually impossible between the towns and villages of the West Bank. According to the Bethlehem-based research group Badil, the West Bank is currently divided into sixty-four pieces, none of them joined, surrounded by forty-six permanent checkpoints and usually more than a hundred roadblocks, and threaded by a road-system which segregates Israelis from Palestinians. According to the Badil report, so far 'Israel's self-declared war on terrorism has left approximately eighteen hundred Palestinians and four hundred Israeli civilians dead, more than twenty thousand Palestinians injured and some eight thousand in Israeli detention centres.'

The future of the Palestinian people is grave. The more Israel clamps down in the Occupied Territories, the more of a breeding ground they become for terror. There were no suicide bombings before the Oslo peace process. They are a new phenomenon which emerged as Israel exerted more and more control over Palestinian lives whilst appearing to offer them more freedom under the Oslo negotiations. The Palestinians I have spoken to feel completely impotent about the determination of their future. The despair is worse than ever before. The terror they experience on a daily basis is ignored in the rhetoric of the global 'war on terror'.

9. Checkpoints and Chances

7 December 2002

The Bethlehem checkpoint has now been closed for the last sixteen days. So have all the other exits and entrances to the town and its surrounding villages. I've been getting in and out under curfew because I use a car which has 'TV' written on its windscreen and windows, rather than the normal bright yellow taxis; the driver is Christian and is prepared to risk being caught breaking curfew. He tells me the Israeli soldiers are more lenient towards Christians than Muslims, suspecting that 'terrorism' comes from the latter. Also, I can afford four times the price I might otherwise pay under normal circumstances, and if we do get stopped, my foreign passport could at the worst mean being arrested for being in a 'closed military zone', but it is just as likely I would get told simply to go back home.

I have not yet encountered a single tank or army jeep in these strange journeys through silent streets. The reinforcing of the curfew here does not seem too tight at the moment, which locals tell me means that the army intends to stay a long time. The ten-kilometre journey to Jerusalem takes double the time as well as the cost. We drive up a different hill miles from the main checkpoint, and at the top I get out and walk over a mud roadblock, then take any vehicle I can pick up down to the main Hebron road. Fantastic views over a beautiful land, I think – ironically – as I walk 'free'.

Some Bethlehemites are breaking curfew at the fringes of the town but most stay indoors as the situation could be volatile. The taxi driver has six children and he told me today that they are going mad inside the house. So Bethlehem sits largely in silence;

sewage smells increase and the garbage of the last sixteen days remains uncollected on the streets. Occasionally we come across a smoking rubbish container. Near Azza refugee camp en route between my flat and the mud roadblock 'exit' there are sometimes burning tyres, set up in defiance and anger by the young people in the camp. If the army do find people on the streets they sometimes use sound-bombs or tear gas to disperse them.

This week was the *Eid al Fitr* festival for the end of Ramadan, the month of charity and fasting, and one of the biggest festivals in the Muslim calendar. My Palestinian friends tell me it has not been a time of celebration this year. Normally everyone would have new clothes and the families would visit each other and break their fast together. This year, it was only possible to get the basics to eat in the two three-hour slots the shops were permitted to open in the lead up to the festival, and, where possible, buy new clothes for the children, if you had enough energy to fight your way through the crowds.

Even when Bethlehem was not under curfew, most residents could still not go anywhere outside the town. Palestinians are now defined by a plastic magnetic card. Everyone who wishes to travel into Israel (including East Jerusalem) from the West Bank has to apply for a permit, and the magnetic identity card is required for a permit to be issued. The application form for the ID costs thirty shekels (more than £4) and can only be filled in at Etzion, the Israeli military bureau, several kilometres south of Bethlehem near Arrub refugee camp. To get there you have to take a taxi to Khadr monastery, then walk three hundred metres, then take another taxi. It takes a week to get the card after filling in the form. When swiped, the card then magically opens up a computer file containing your personal history since 1967: date of birth, marital status, children, address, job, religion, time in prison if you've done some . . . The card needs renewing every year. Then you can start applying for a permit to travel. Since May 2002, Palestinians wanting to travel within the West Bank need special permits as well, which are hard, if not often impossible, to obtain.

Fatma at the Bethlehem checkpoint

Fatma is sixty-five and lives in Beit Jala, a neighbouring town of Bethlehem. I found her on Tuesday 12 November at half past eight in the morning on the Bethlehem side of the checkpoint. She had breached the line of people waiting to have their identity cards examined and was getting in a strop with the soldier who wouldn't let her through. There was a certain amount of amusement involved. She was adamant that she had a hospital appointment to go to in Jerusalem for her eyes. The soldier said she hadn't got the right permit to get through. Fatma sat down on the ground in defiance, holding her hospital card and unleashing her anger. They both knew they were fighting at the limits of a system.

I quietly asked the soldier if she looked like a terrorist. He replied, properly of course, that he had orders not to let people through without the correct permit, but agreed to speak to his commander a few hundred metres further up. The answer came back by phone: no, she couldn't go through. Somehow, Fatma and I managed to persuade him to walk with us up to the kiosk with the next level of soldiers to confirm what he said he'd been told.

I was allowed through after showing my passport, but Fatma wasn't. I told them she said she had a hospital appointment. They said no. I told them that they could check her bags for weapons. The soldier called his superior over, still holding my passport. 'Can't she just come with me? She is not causing you any problems,' I said. Silence. 'I could be more of a problem than she is,'

I suggested. Shortly afterwards, he said abruptly in Hebrew, 'Go.' Confusion. 'And can she go too?' Impatience. 'Yes.' So we went through, Fatma tripping up on a rough piece of concrete as we clutched hands through the checkpoint.

My reward was her tight grip, a few kisses and a torrent of blessings. Fatma's hospital appointment card was from February 2002 so she was a bit out of date. I asked her, once round the checkpoint, what she was really going to do? 'Sell these,' she said, pointing to bags of green leaves and olives. She told me her thirty-five-year-old son was sick, and he had four children.

Checkpoints have become a system to keep an entire population subjugated, controlled and humiliated. What is more, the army knows that thousands of people throughout the West Bank circumvent the checkpoints, often at risk to their own lives. Jewish settlers, meanwhile, drive by on roads throughout the West Bank, never having to negotiate a checkpoint, and perhaps in many cases oblivious to their very existence.

10. Across the Divide

14 December 2002

'*Mamnu attajawal! Mamnu attajawal!* It is forbidden to be outside!'

Broadcast from Israeli army jeeps and tanks, this is the order under which the residents of Bethlehem have been living since 22 November, leaving 160,000 people effectively under house arrest – 60,000 in Bethlehem town, 100,000 in Beit Sahur, Beit Jala and outlying villages. Not only is Bethlehem 're-occupied' territory: it is also under twenty-four-hour curfew, and, in addition, is also currently a 'closed military zone'.

Ten kilometres to the north lies Jerusalem – Yerushalaym – or Al Quds (the holy) to Muslims. The contrasts are stark. East Jerusalem was alive and buzzing for the *Eid* last week. Fresh fruit and vegetables were available and thousands of Jerusalemite Palestinians came to shop and to pray. Shopping malls, traffic

Women in Black demonstrate in West Jerusalem

lights that work, green parks, cinema, theatre, classical concerts all suggest that life in West Jerusalem is also normal. But beneath the surface, some cracks appear.

'I either extinguish myself or feel permanently immoral,' said my Israeli friend, Ainat, as we sat in a café in West Jerusalem last week. A rather staggering statement, I thought, given that the café we were sitting in had previously been the scene of a suicide bombing. But this was the dilemma she felt in simply being Israeli – trying to reconcile the love of her country with its political actions. She believes that Israel shores up its own existence at the expense of the Palestinian people. I met Ainat earlier this year protesting against Israel's occupation of the West Bank and Gaza with Women in Black – a group who stand every Friday from noon until one o'clock on a main intersection in West Jerusalem with placards in Hebrew and English saying 'Stop the Occupation'.

It would be hard to stop the occupation. It is so concreted in. The Jewish settlements, with the lattice of Jewish-only roads connecting them, hold the West Bank and Gaza in a cancerous grip, fragmenting the land into dozens of 'bantustans' which stifle life in the Palestinian areas between them. So one solution to this conflict would be for Israel to pull out. The Palestinians I know would be content just to have these lands returned to them and live next to the Israeli state – as long as that means they control their own water and electricity supply, borders, air space and all that having a real sovereign country means. After all, these lands constitute just twenty-two per cent of what was Palestine under the British Mandate. Most Palestinian violence is an expression of despair and hatred at having their lives occupied for thirty-five years and their every movement controlled.

The vast majority of Israelis either have no idea what is happening a few miles from their homes or simply don't want to know. Even if they want to, they are legally barred from entering the Palestinian towns and cities to see for themselves. They live with the real fear that a bus may explode anywhere and at any time. They don't know that fifty per cent of the Palestinian population of three million lives on some form of food assistance because of the Israeli imposed closures. Perhaps equally many Palestinians are unaware that the cost of the war in the Occupied Territories means that one hundred thousand Israeli families are expected to fall under the poverty line within a year, as a result of cutbacks on welfare spending in the current national budget. Yet the terror felt in Tel Aviv or Jerusalem is the same terror felt amongst the streets of Gaza, Hebron or the mud alleys of Deheishe refugee camp. All are residential areas and all are inhabited by innocent civilians.

The 'civilians' on either side are not always so different. Behind the word 'Israel' lies a vast array of cultures. Fred, my colleague at the Israeli Committee Against House Demolitions (ICAHD), was brought up in the United States but his mother is a Palestinian Jew. Yes, a Palestinian Jew. That is, a Jewish woman who lived in Palestine before 1948 and spoke Palestinian Arabic. At home she spoke Yiddish, in the synagogue Hebrew, and to the British during the Mandate, English. She also picked up Turkish from her father who spoke it out of necessity when Palestine was ruled by the Ottomans. But for his giveaway pronunciation of 'r', Fred sounds American.

When buying a bagel next to the ICAHD office in West Jerusalem the other day, I noticed that the shopkeeper looked

'Arab' except he wore a *yarmulka* (skull cap). We spoke English, I tried the only words of Hebrew I knew . . . and eventually couldn't resist trying some Arabic. 'Ah!' he said grinning and launched into a fast Arabic reply. 'How come you speak Arabic?' I asked. 'My father is Moroccan' he said with pride . . . Another Jewish Arab.

Even though Israel's existence is assured politically and militarily with its nuclear capability, the demographic war is still on. Prime Minister Ariel Sharon has called for a million new immigrants in the next decade. To encourage them, each family of four immigrants receives a grant of about US \$8,000 in their first year in addition to free one-way tickets to Israel, rent subsidies or cheaper mortgage rates for five years, customs rights on imported goods for three years, and free health insurance and Hebrew study for six months. This now applies not only to Jews from the former USSR, Ethiopia, Argentina, France but also North America.

To her disapproval, Ainat's brother bought land in the West Bank. It was cheap and he was given a government grant to entice him to buy. But since the Intifada broke out he has not felt secure enough to live there.

11. From A to B: West Bank Journeys

14 December 2002

It is seven in the morning, and I am writing this at a checkpoint. We are in one taxi in a string of about a hundred waiting to pass through what amounts to a few large stone blocks and two gates in the middle of the road. I am way up in the north of the West Bank near the village of Tayasir, not far from Jenin. We left Tulkarem this morning (Saturday) at half past five and arrived here an hour later. We – that is, Jo, my Quaker colleague, four Palestinan students and a man – are trying to get to Ramallah. If you happen

Fire to keep warm at Tayasir checkpoint

to know the geography of the West Bank, you might ask why we are now near Jenin – north-east – having come from Tulkarem in the west in order to get to Ramallah in the south. This is West Bank travel, West Bank style, the black-magical mystery tour. We have to travel in a massive loop through Jericho and the Jordan Valley because Palestinian cars (with green number plates) cannot travel on the main West Bank trunk road south. Under normal circumstances the journey would have taken just over an hour.

Now it's eight o'clock, and we're still here. The girls in the taxi are saying that they have to tell the checkpoint soldiers that they are going to Jericho, rather than Ramallah. They don't have a permit to enter Ramallah, where they study. Permits are hard to get and cost money. As Palestinians they are required to apply for permission to travel between their towns. Many don't bother. A man in the taxi office said at five this morning, 'Why should we apply to Israelis for permission to travel on our own roads?' Of course, under these conditions travel documents get forged. Forged ones cost a lot. Genuine ones even more. Imagine British citizens having to pay to apply for permission to travel between London and Birmingham, and then having to travel there via Brighton on muddy roads with broken tarmac. The girls imply that the soldiers know that they are really going to Ramallah. It's a game.

Another half hour passes. There are old people, young people, sick people and children packed into these taxis. The sun is coming up and more cars join the queue. It's freezing up here in these beautiful hills. Having warmed ourselves on a fire that some of the men have just built on the roadside, Jo and I have just wandered down to the checkpoint, as none of the cars are moving. We couldn't see any soldiers, and the cars were stationary.

As soon as we breached the checkpoint, a soldier appeared and called us to halt. Another one came out to speak to us. 'Why aren't you letting any of these cars through?' we asked. 'Look, we have to check these people,' he said. 'I can't work if the people keep getting out of their cars. If they stay inside the cars, I'll let them pass.' When I looked round most people were in their cars, patiently waiting. Some had been there since half past five in the

My travelling companions at Tayasir checkpoint

morning. It was only those out of sight from the middle to the end of the queue who were spilling out of their vehicles to stretch, or to play with their children or warm themselves. Jo stayed near the soldier and he started checking passes and letting the people through. I talked to the people in the cars to tell them what the soldier said.

At nine o'clock an old couple walk to the front of the queue. They're told to stop. The man, wearing a Palestinian headdress, sits down on the ground in the middle of the checkpoint. The soldier says: 'It's very simple, if someone is sick, they can come and tell me and I'll let them through.' The old man was apparently due to have an eye operation in Jerusalem. He was carrying his x-rays with him to prove it. The frustration in our car is now rising and we are hungry.

It was pitch black when we left Tulkarem this morning under curfew. It wasn't until it got a bit lighter that I asked where we were and got a map out. We've been here three and a half hours – now it's ten o'clock. The cars are trickling through. Time enough for other thoughts. Yesterday, we stopped at Zeita village near Tulkarem to look at massive groundwork preparations for the new Israeli 'security fence'. We were drinking tea with a dozen men, including the mayor of Zeita and a local business man, when we heard the drone of Apache helicopters. Suddenly, the atmosphere changed. Our friends said they knew the Israelis were looking for someone on their wanted list in Tulkarem. The Apaches were covering a ground operation from the air. It was eerie and we all kept looking at the Apaches a few kilometres away. Muhammad, who was showing us around, got news on his mobile that soldiers and tanks were surrounding a house in Nur Shams refugee camp, inside Tulkarem town. Sure enough, in last night's news, we learned the wanted person (a man in his early twenties) was dead, a 'martyr', and six others had been injured, one seriously, in the operation. We heard the tanks still moving around late last night, and a curfew was imposed on the town.

Ten past ten. We've just seen that there are at least a dozen soldiers behind the barbed wire of their makeshift office. Why aren't

more of them manning the checkpoint? I could certainly do with
a wash and some breakfast, now. But I think we have another hour
and a half ahead of us before we reach Ramallah. The girls have
just joked that it would be quicker for us all to get to Britain than it
is to get to Ramallah. (Actually, when I think about it, this is true.)

Eleven minutes later we're finally through the checkpoint
after nearly four hours of waiting. The soldier has just checked all
our passports and documents. He addressed each of the girls by
their name, and asked where they were going and why. 'Jericho,
for a visit,' was the reply each time. He didn't ask further. He didn't
probe. These questions were nothing to do with security. Forged
documents were not scrutinised. The car wasn't even checked for
explosives. None of this pertains to the security of Israel. These
people are travelling within the West Bank. I asked the soldier
why he was keeping us all waiting so long when his fellow-soldiers
at the checkpoint could be helping. 'They have other work to do,'
he said. What other work? I wonder. Under international law these
checkpoints are illegal. Freedom of movement is a human right.
Checkpoints are punishing an entire nation for the sins of a few.
When people ask what I am doing here, and I mention human
rights, it seems to be a big joke. 'Human rights?' they laugh. 'There
aren't any. We are animals.'

By eleven o'clock I understand why we had to leave so early
from Tulkarem. I feel tense, tired and irritable. Having laughed
with relief at getting through the checkpoint, the girls are now
silent. Comfort-stop just before Jericho. We pass the rolling hills
of the 'Judean' wilderness on one side and the fertile lands in the
Jordan Valley on the other – lands which Israel has fenced off and
reoccupied during the Oslo negotiations, designating them as the
unreachable 'Area C'. There are now many Jewish settlements in
the Jordan Valley. But this is all West Bank, Palestinian land.

Steep climb, half an hour later, up from the Jordan Valley into
the desert hills. A driver coming in the other direction has just
flashed at our driver to say that the army up ahead have erected a
checkpoint, so we've turned round, turned off the main road, and
are driving across a stony hillside. Two other taxis who got the

message are in front of us. This is unbelievable. I can hardly type for the bumps. The car doesn't sound too good either. But we are on a clear mud track, obviously used by other vehicles to avoid the soldiers. This is just a barren rocky hill. There is a Jewish settlement on the horizon. That probably explains the checkpoint.

Around eleven forty we rejoin the main road, and ten minutes before midday we finally arrive at Qalandiya checkpoint in Ramallah. I go in the direction of Jerusalem – a city forbidden to all Palestinians except those with a Jerusalem identity card. So, it's goodbye to the girls, my travelling companions for the last six and a half hours, on a journey that could (and should) only have taken one.

12. Bethlehem on its Knees

20 December 2002

It's raining in Bethlehem today. Grey-laden skies, strong winds, and torrents of water pouring down the valleys. The people, however, are rushing up the valleys, up into town. Yes, the curfew has been lifted for a few hours.

A mad scramble as cars jam up in the narrow lanes. The pressure is on: to restock basic food supplies, see the doctor, get to work, meet the retailer to keep the shop stocked, get to the bank, hold vital meetings that have been postponed too long, take exams at university, pay overdue bills if there's extra cash ... oh, and take the children to school. It's Friday and there shouldn't be any school for Muslims but some teachers opened up today to make up for lost time – that lost time being most of the last twenty-nine days since curfew was imposed.

This is the Christmas rush. Not a rush for Christmas. Surviving has taken precedence over Christmas. Everything has to be accomplished, despite traffic, crowds and rain, before five this afternoon. That's really going to be CLOSING TIME. And that's only if the Israeli army doesn't renege on its promise.

Bethlehem: Old Quarter

At quarter to eight on Wednesday morning, fifteen minutes before the curfew was due to be lifted (as announced the previous evening), with children dressed ready for school, and many people already on their way to work, the army changed its mind. '*Mamnu attajawal!* Forbidden to be outside!' – words that every three-year-old Palestinian can now imitate – were broadcast again from Israeli jeeps. That same day, the army found an old lady and a young man outside in Star Street, one of the oldest streets leading up to Manger Square. They took them in their jeep to Beit Sahur – the neighbouring town (the traditional site of the Shepherds' Fields), and made them walk back to Bethlehem on foot, a punishment for breaking curfew. I have seen several people left stranded in their cars after the army has taken their keys from them. Unable to lock their vehicles to prevent theft, they have to stay there for hours, and sometimes overnight, until their keys are returned.

Meanwhile, the apparent reasons for the curfew's reinforcement seem to get ever more tenuous. Every day the Israeli army arrests 'wanted' men, or rather their friends and families, in and around Bethlehem. Today, I went with staff from the Arab Education Institute to visit a family whose house in Duha, Bethlehem, was almost demolished on Tuesday (17 December). The young couple with their three-month-old daughter awoke at four in the morning to the sound of a bulldozer outside. Soldiers entered the house, and told the family to go to their neighbours. Because their late father Hussein Ibrahim 'Isa was a well-known peace activist who worked with Israeli peace groups and the Americans, his daughter called the American consulate at eight in the morning, just as the bulldozers began to rip up their front garden. The consulate managed to obtain an immediate injunction from the Supreme Court to stop the destruction.

Only then did the army's reason for wanting to demolish the house become clear. Two days ago a man on the Israeli wanted list, with known connections to the Tanzim militant faction, was arrested along with two friends. He had rented an apartment from Hussein's son for just two days, using a false name. The son, Ibrahim, had no idea who his tenant was, and only the fame of his father, who died two years ago, managed to save his house. This is an unusual victory. Many more families in similar situations have no recourse to the law, and no connections to the West.

There are very few signs of Christmas around Bethlehem. At night the streets are dark, because previous military incursions have stripped out their lighting. A few neon crosses are lit up here and there as a sign that Christians are living nearby, somewhere. In the darkness strong Christian voices are speaking. On a local TV station the other night the Latin Patriarch, Michel Sabbah, who lives in Jerusalem, urged the Christian community to celebrate Christmas in spite of the circumstances:

> As for the siege and the humiliation imposed on the Palestinians of Bethlehem itself and on all the Palestinian towns and villages, and the demolition of houses and the killing of people, all these measures push us rather to renew our courage, our hope and

our love even to those who make hard our life. Therefore we have to pray, may God put an end to all that and give us instead justice, dignity and love. The present difficulties will not compel us to cancel our feasts. (18 December)

Local peace organisations are currently deciding what to do when the Patriarch makes his traditional visit from Jerusalem to Bethlehem on 24 December to pray at the Church of the Nativity and herald the start of Christmas. If there is a curfew, should they break it? If Israel allows Bethlehem to open again for a few hours, should they boycott it?

Of course any 'favours' granted by Israel to the Christian population would be a welcome respite to the Muslim majority who were forced to hold their celebrations behind closed doors two weeks ago. Beyond Israel's political game of treating the religious communities differently, however, lies a grave humanitarian crisis which does not make religious distinctions.

Down the road in Deheishe refugee camp in Bethlehem, a Muslim family I sat with this week has had no income for two years. Ahmad, the father, looked harrowed and tired. He had worked for twenty years as a carpenter for an Israeli company in Jerusalem, just the other side of the main Bethlehem checkpoint. It was the wrong side and he lost his job when the peace talks collapsed and the Intifada started. Their savings have now been used up, and there are no other breadwinners. Their ten children are still of school age, and they cannot afford the increased transport costs to get their children to school through the maze of checkpoints and roadblocks which surround Bethlehem and its outlying villages even on open days.

They, along with fifty per cent of Palestinians in the Occupied Territories, are now the recipients of food handouts from the UN. The average pack consists of fifty kilograms of flour, five kilograms of rice, five more each of sugar and lentils, a kilogram of whole milk powder and two litres of sunflower oil. Fresh produce is also a casualty of the checkpoints. As a result, malnutrition is increasing.

Maysa, the eighteen-year-old daughter, a university student, looked painfully thin. She sang to a dusty cassette of Arabic songs and only occasionally joined our conversation. 'When there is school, I eat. When there isn't, I don't,' she said, with an air of defiance. The strains of living under occupation and closure are painfully apparent.

Interestingly, the occupation is not only affecting Palestinians' eating habits. There are also changes in Israeli food consumption. In Jerusalem, just ten kilometres north of Bethlehem, fast food is more popular than ever before. When an Israeli family I was with last week dialled for pizza, the delivery man appeared just two short minutes after our order was placed. With families now reluctant to dine out in the restaurants and cafés of West Jerusalem for fear of attacks, the fast-food take-away industry is doing well. Beyond this, there is no comparison with an existence under occupation. The rest of life in Jerusalem goes on as normal, whereas in Bethlehem it has been brought to a standstill.

Tonight Bethlehem is far from silent. Everyone is indoors waiting for the next breath of freedom, and the Christians are certainly wondering whether they can go to church at Christmas. But this is the bleak midwinter and the winds are raging, raging around the valleys. They are expressing a fact: Bethlehem is on its knees. Not through the adoration of the Christ Child but because it is being humiliated and crushed.

13. No Room at the Inn

31 December 2002

Three days before Christmas, a bulldozer started hammering repeatedly at the roof of a house until it collapsed. It was the house of Jawdi Jaber, brother of Atta (see report 3, 'The Battle of the Hilltops'). The house was nearly complete: I saw work in progress three weeks ago en route from Hebron to Jerusalem. Jawdi received no demolition order and was stunned when the bulldozer came on 2 December. He was given only five minutes' warning and many possessions, including his fridge and TV, were destroyed along with

Christmas Eve in Manger Square

the house. He had been building for a year, and had been saving for years before that. His father's house is crowded: his parents live in one room, his sister and family in the other two. The new house was a dream. Kawkab and his other daughters were inconsolable as they returned from school and saw what had happened.

I just called him tonight from Bethlehem while writing this, to ask what he would do now, having lost all his assets and without recourse to insurance. He told me how he and his five children are now living in a cave built into the rock on which his father's house stands. 'I pray to God to give me more power to make another house. Maybe I need ten or twelve years,' he said. 'The Israelis already took my mountain,' he added, referring to the orchard he had spent a decade cultivating on top of the hill his family had farmed for centuries, and which the Jewish settlement of Harsina recently confiscated. Jawdi wondered what he had done wrong. He had fasted through Ramadan and he prays five times every day. The cost of the house he was building, he said, was $40,000.

Nobody can say exactly why his home was targeted. But it could be related to the fact that on 18 December the Israeli High

Court extended the restraining order preventing the Israeli army from demolishing fifteen Palestinian homes in the heart of Hebron. Jewish settlers in Hebron want these houses to be demolished so that they don't have to go through any Palestinian area between their settlement and the Tomb of the Patriarchs (or Ibrahimi Mosque) in the centre of Hebron. But while this case is on hold, a wave of other house demolitions is taking place, and Jawdi's house, unfortunately, was among those picked out.

Manger Square in Bethlehem has neither a Christmas tree nor lights. It did, however, provide the backdrop to many signs protesting at the impossible conditions the Bethlehemites are living through. 'Silent Night . . . Holy Night??' read one poster. The Latin Patriarch, Michel Sabbah, proceeded to pass through, in drizzle and cold, on his way to the Church of the Nativity to begin Christmas in earnest. During midnight mass at St Catherine's he strongly criticised Israel's occupation of the West Bank and Gaza as the main cause of the suffering of the Palestinian people.

Tidings of joy were palpably thin amongst the Christian family with whom I ate Christmas lunch. Having lost nearly all the customers in his furniture store during December because of the curfew, one son could only regard the opening hours for the festival with suspicion as he contemplated his business going down the drain. Sure enough, at three o'clock on Boxing Day afternoon, *Mamnu Attajawal,* 'You are forbidden to be outside', was yet again broadcast from Israeli jeeps around Manger Square and tear gas heralded the next period of home confinement.

This morning – New Year's Eve – I spent several hours distributing leaflets in the streets of Bethlehem advertising the Justice & Peace March at three o'clock, an event initiated last year by the local peace organisations. Bethlehem has been open twenty-four hours a day for the last few days. 'Can we throw rocks?' joked one man. 'I can't wait to smell the gas,' said another. Many were glad something was happening and promised to come. One person asked why a foreigner was handing out the posters. The answer is, many young people from the town who would have distributed posters feel less comfortable doing so this year as the situation in Bethlehem – after six months of total closure and five military incursions during the last year – is ten times worse than it was on 31 December 2001. Many are afraid that a peaceful demonstration will turn sour or, alternatively, they think that there's no point.

However, several hundred people turned out. The Latin Patriarch, and Anglican, Orthodox and other religious dignitaries arrived in a fleet from Jerusalem, and our march towards the checkpoint began. 'Open Jerusalem' and 'End the Occupation' banners were held above the heads of a peaceful crowd as we advanced down the streets. Long before we reached the checkpoint, however, a line of Israeli jeeps and soldiers was barring the way. Small boys amongst us – mostly from the refugee camps nearby – immediately got excited and began to overtake the dignitaries. Internationals and organisers tried to stop them to avoid any provocation on either side. After some negotiation we were allowed to proceed a bit further but got stopped again by more jeeps and soldier reinforcements. So the inter-faith prayers were held there and then by the different community organisations and dignitaries, confronting a line of soldiers in the middle of the road. The boys crept forward, fascinated by the soldiers' uniforms and guns, and got pushed back. Songs and hymns were sung, led by the leaders through a microphone, and speeches delivered about seeking peace and an end to occupation. Thankfully the march ended peacefully, the crowd began to retreat, and – with a lot of persuasion – so did the smaller boys.

14. The Shooting Gallery

9 January 2003

They live between bullets. They live on the edge of existence. They live in a refugee camp. And almost every day one of them dies. Last night it was Ayman, a man in his thirties. I saw his blood on the stones this morning. He will never again frequent the sandy track

Gaza: demolished building

– or 'shooting gallery' – in which he died. But his five children still have to negotiate it.

A world apart from the rolling hills of Bethlehem and the West Bank, Gaza lies on the edge of the Egyptian sands. Dusty, rural, littered with date palms. Over a million people are packed into the Strip, 40km (25 miles) long, 8km (5 miles) wide. Three-quarters of them are refugees. Around seventy thousand of them live in Khan Younis refugee camp.

The January sun was warm as the asphalt road dissolved into sand under our feet. Hordes of children started to follow us. Ismail, my host, told them to go home. He got nervous as we approached a corner. 'You can see the military camp?' In the far distance was an earth mound with what looked to me like a tank facing the alleyway. Urged to great caution, we walked round the corner. Houses and shacks on both sides were riddled with bullet holes and pockmarked by tank shells.

Gaza: inhabitants
of a demolished house

We found Ali, a man in his forties, in a sandy lane off this 'shooting gallery'. He was watching his children playing. The smallest of his boys rode a bike through empty rooms. 'If they start shooting we fling ourselves down here,' he said, pointing to a room on the other side of the house. The trouble is, the shooting can come from all directions.

This western edge of Khan Younis refugee camp is surrounded on three sides by the enclave of Jewish settlements called Gush Katif. Jewish settlers, surrounded by a massive wall of grey concrete slabs, live right next to Palestinian refugees. Forty per cent of this tiny strip of land has been taken by Jewish settlements. From Ali's windows I saw the skeleton of a demolished apartment block, the roof slanting downwards. Next to it, piles of stone from collapsed houses with the odd piece of colour peeping out. These home demolitions create a convenient buffer zone between the security wall of the settlement, which nearby Israeli military encampments jealously guard, and the rest of the refugee camp. The camp long pre-dates the settlements, however. Palestinian refugees fled cities such as Jaffa during the war of 1948 and came to Gaza.

'We are refugees yet they take our children, our homes, our lives!' wailed a woman dressed in black, who ran out to tell me that she has lost two of her four sons in the last sixty days.

Near the piles of demolished homes, I met a lady who still goes back to the shell of her home at night. 'Where else are we supposed to sleep?'

A few hundred metres down the road, next to the settlement wall, we came to a scene reminiscent of sub-Saharan Africa: a group of some fifty women and men sitting under the shade of a makeshift hut. They were waiting to go home, back to Mawasi, a narrow strip of fruit-laden land, a home of sorts for seven and a half thousand people. The checkpoint opens and closes at random; equally arbitrary are the rules that dictate who can go in and out. One recent law apparently says that no one under the age of fifty-four can come or go. Split into two separated parts, Mawasi possesses two small health clinics and one school.

Because Mawasi was designated as 'Area C' under the Oslo Accords, the Palestinian Ministry of Health cannot work there, so clinics are run by military medical services. One woman told me she was trying to get her daughter-in-law back to her husband in Mawasi. The daughter was nursing her one-and-a-half-year-old child. They had been here five days running and were sleeping in a nearby mosque at night. Other women clutched medicine they had bought in Khan Younis to take back to their families. A man said that he used to be a fisherman. But most of the Gaza coastline is now out of bounds to Palestinian fishermen, leaving just a six kilometre square from which the Gazans can obtain their fish.

The whole area is watched carefully at night. Israeli forces frequently fire shells into the camp at the slightest sound. Any movement at night by the residents is detected via infrared cameras. This is how Ayman died. He heard the sound of an Israeli tank nearby and peeped round the corner of the shooting gallery to see where it was. He was shot instantly in the head. The night before another man, Majid, also in his thirties ('One of my best and most brilliant students,' said my host), encountered the same fate, putting his head round the corner of the main street near the demolished houses to locate where a tank was. He has now been pronounced clinically dead.

The nightly raids go on. Khan Younis has one of the highest Intifada casualty rates. Ali thinks his house will soon be demolished. He no longer sleeps there at night with his eight children but rents somewhere further away. But the children go on playing in the shooting gallery during the day. Their lives are in danger simply because of their proximity to a Jewish settlement which imposed itself on their land. A longstanding question in the minds of many Israelis and Palestinians since this second Intifada broke out is, 'Can the settlements remain if there is to be peace?'

'Tell the people of the UK, we just want peace,' said Amna, my host's wife, as I left Khan Younis. 'We welcome anyone – Europeans, Americans, even Israelis. All we want is peace.'

15. 'May God Make Great Your Reward'

15 January 2003

I've learned to say *Allah 'athar ajrakum* ('May God make great your reward'). This is what you say to the mourning relatives of any Palestinian who was killed by the Israeli army. This week in Bethlehem, Tariq, a seventeen-year-old refugee, died in Aida camp, not far from where I live. He was apparently throwing stones at the Israeli army, and was certainly not armed. His mother looked pale, sitting in the corner of the front room of her house, as people poured in to offer their condolences.

Tariq is considered a martyr. He died for the national cause. His funeral – last Saturday – was therefore a national event and got screened on Palestinian TV. Anyone from the camp or the adjoining area can come and pay respects to his family. His mother will sit

Poster of Tariq

for three days receiving visitors, many of whom she has never met and will probably never meet again. The Arab Education Institute, with other local Bethlehem peace groups, made a solidarity visit. Women gathered in Tariq's house, and the men somewhere else. We sat in silence. We were offered cups of bitter Arabic coffee, and a small sweet each. The narrow house is perched on a concrete plinth on the corner of an alleyway. Aida camp – like most camps – is a series of garbage-strewn concrete alleyways, too narrow for cars, cut off from access to the main road by barbed wire, with Israeli army posts stationed at its entrances. The refugee camps in Bethlehem (Aida, Deheishe and Azza) are isolated within the town. They have frequently experienced more of the heavy-handed behaviour of the Israeli army, including sound-bombs, tear gas, house searches in the middle of the night, and ugly language being broadcast after dark from Israeli jeeps. This is the world in which Tariq, one of the 'children of the stones', lived.

Tariq, like sixty thousand other residents, could not leave Bethlehem because, in the first place, he couldn't obtain a permit; secondly, even if he had a permit allowing him to go somewhere else, a new law was introduced by Israel this week prohibiting any Palestinian under the age of thirty-five from moving between towns and villages in the West Bank and from leaving the Occupied Territories to get into Israel, even if they have the right permit *and a foreign passport*. (The only exceptions are Palestinians under four months old.)

Thirdly, Bethlehem is now closed again. For the last week a rumour has been spreading amongst locals and taxi drivers that on 15 January (today), all West Bank towns would be closed for a long time. And the rumour, it turns out, was correct. At five this morning, curfew was announced. Whether in response to the Tel Aviv suicide bombing, or the Israeli election period culminating on 28 January, no one quite knows. Many universities have been shut this week across the West Bank. So the closures are tightening here and no one can move.

A standard response from the Israelis I have met, when I question why Palestinians have to live this way, is best captured in a conversation I had with a volunteer Israeli reservist, aged fifty-four, whom I met at the Bethlehem checkpoint a few weeks ago. We started talking when I saw a soldier, one of his colleagues, shouting aggressively into the face of a Palestinian man who had already shown him his identity and gone through the checkpoint. The man was told to wait. I walked through, after having my passport looked at by the same soldier. I hesitated, turned back and asked the reservist if he could explain to me what was happening. It was exactly the time of *Iftar* – breaking the Ramadan fast at sunset – and there were not many people about. The reservist said they had their reasons to be suspicious about the Palestinian, and started off at quite a loud pitch (I'll put my responses in italics).

'We Israelis are getting attacked on all sides and we have a right to defend ourselves. I have three kids and our people are being blown up on buses. They kill women and children in their beds [a reference to a recent Palestinian attack on a Jewish settlement].' *Yes, and the Israeli army kill innocent women and children every day in the Occupied Territories.*

'That is why I offer to come here to help at the checkpoint. My colleague was not being violent. Did you see any violence?' *Yes, verbal violence, and aggressive behaviour.*

'Look, two years ago [at Camp David] our then prime minister Ehud Barak offered the Palestinians a state and they rejected it.' *Yes, it may have seemed generous but it wasn't. All the real control remained in Israeli hands – borders, water, airspace, and the land was fragmented in pieces. It would have been impossible to build a sovereign state which could have worked economically and socially.*

'Arafat deliberately intended the violence of the Intifada.' *The Palestinians had waited through seven years of negotiations to see their lives improve. But Israel went on building settlements on their land, making their lives more difficult, and denying them many basic human rights. The Intifada was provoked by the visit of Ariel Sharon to the most sacred Holy Muslim sites. Palestinians protested, Israel shot many dead.*

'In 1967 the Palestinians wanted to push us into the sea. We have to defend ourselves.' *Yes, but the Palestinians I talk to accept Israel's right to exist. The Oslo negotiations were based on an affirmation of Israel's right to exist. It was the Palestinians who made the biggest concession at the start of the Oslo negotiations – to build their state on just twenty-two per cent of Mandate Palestine. Israel is one of the most powerful nuclear countries in the world, and is backed by the world's superpower. Where's the equivalence?*

Then the reservist said, in a quieter tone:

'Look, I would shake hands with them. They can live in their own state alongside us . . . I'm sorry for raising my voice towards you.'

We ended up thanking each other for talking, and (I'm afraid) I left the Palestinian man sitting there waiting for his fate.

Conversations like this help me understand the gulf symbolised by the checkpoint. On one side, life goes on pretty much as normal. But the devastating suicide attacks, killing innocent civilians, are pushing many Israelis to relinquish ideas of peace and surrendering territory. (Ironically, some of those killed in the Tel Aviv bombing were non-Jewish migrant workers who have taken the place of Palestinians banned from working in Israel.)

On the other side, every aspect of life – eating, working, moving, education – is becoming impossible for all three million Palestinians. Over twelve hundred Palestinians were killed by the Israeli army in the Occupied Territories in 2002, and nearly ten thousand wounded. Many Bethlehemites tell me they want to leave with me, when I come back to the UK. They are demoralised, and some of the younger generation are prepared, like Tariq, to throw stones.

16. Division of the Promised Land

20 January 2003

It costs US $1million per kilometre. It is being built in the name of security. When complete, it will be three hundred and fifty kilometres long. This is the new Berlin Wall of the Middle East. The Israeli government is building what it terms a 'security fence' or 'separation barrier' to separate Israel from the West Bank. The 'fence' is no less than forty metres wide, and in places forms an eight metre high wall with trenches, wire fences armed with electronic sensors, barbed wire, and surveillance cameras and security patrols to detect anything which approaches. It is to segregate Palestinians

Bulldozers preparing the ground for the 'security fence' near Jayyous

from Israelis and to keep Palestinian gunmen and suicide bombers out of Israel. There seems to be something illogical, however, in the way it is being built. Instead of running along the 'Green Line' (1949 armistice lines) the barrier is beginning to wind its way several kilometres into West Bank land, right up to the houses of Palestinian towns separating them from the land they own.

Jayyous, a rural West Bank town with three thousand inhabitants, has thirteen thousand dunums of land (one *dunum* equals one thousand square metres, or a quarter of an acre). Once completed, the 'fence' will cut off seventy-two per cent of the land of Jayyous, leaving nine thousand *dunums* as a sort of no man's land six kilometres deep between the Green Line and the fence. Being a border town, many residents of Jayyous used to work in Israel, but since the labour market has been closed to Palestinians for the last two years, over seventy per cent of the people now rely entirely on agriculture as their source of income, producing tomatoes, cucumbers, olives and citrus fruits. Even people with non-agricultural jobs often depend partially on crops such as olive trees to supplement their income. It doesn't take much adding up to work

Bulldozed olive trees, replanted by the farmers

out that the security 'fence' will mean the loss of income to over half of Jayyous's already impoverished population.

Israel's need for security is a real one. The twin suicide bombings in Tel Aviv on 5 January not only brought a terrible, futile carnage, but served to amplify that need. Whether the separation barrier will prevent such attacks remains to be seen. Causing many Palestinians to lose their livelihoods will certainly not enhance Israel's security. Jayyous is not the only small town to suffer. In the first hundred and fifteen kilometres, twenty-three villages will lose part or all of their land (ninety thousand *dunums*) totalling two per cent of the West Bank. Overall, thirty groundwater wells will be in the no man's land, meaning that many villages will lose their main source of water.

'For us, it is just a matter of stealing more land and water to force Palestinians out of Palestine,' said Ghassan, our host who works for the Palestinian Ministry of Agriculture. Israel says that it will put gates in to allow Palestinian farmers to continue tending their crops. 'We are not optimistic about those gates. Israel will control them. We feel our agriculture will be destroyed. We have many greenhouses which are like babies . . . needing constant care and attentions.' Ghassan added. The gates will mean yet more Israeli control over the lives of Palestinians in their own land.

'The security fence is a government non-decision,' said an Israeli academic we met recently. He described it as the government's attempt, under pressure, to navigate a path through contradictory Israeli views: most Israelis understandably desire security and some see the erection of the barrier as a solution; others have the lingering fantasy of the Israel which stretches right up to the Jordan River, encompassing the whole West Bank. Still others are concerned at the terrible economic effect that the cost of the barrier is having on the rest of the country, in which the gap between rich and poor has never been wider. Perhaps reflecting the internal Israeli division on this issue, the government, so far, has given budget approval for just one hundred kilometres.

Walls and barriers may sometimes be pragmatic but they also symbolise a failure to communicate. Choosing the term 'fence' is an attempt to soften the approach and mask the controversial and horrendous reality of what is happening on the ground. In the same way Israel calls Jewish settlements in the Occupied Territories 'neighbourhoods', blurring the line between what under international law is Israel, and what is occupied by Israel. Will the security barrier help, ironically, to create a border of a sovereign Palestinian state? How will the Jewish settlers react trapped inside the West Bank, on the wrong side?

Azmi Bishara, a Palestinian Member of the Israeli Knesset (parliament), recently fought a case to ask the State to choose a different route for a section in Kufr Aqab, near Jerusalem, being built extremely close to Palestinian residential areas. The case argued that private land was being confiscated to build the barrier on this route, and if anyone attempted to infiltrate it, Palestinian civilians would have their lives endangered by their proximity, and they could even have their houses demolished as a result of any conflict, as has happened frequently in Gaza. The Israeli committee focusing on the Law to Seize Land in Times of Emergency (enacted in 1949) rejected the appeal, arguing that the right of Israeli citizens to life exceeded the rights of property ownership and that the barrier is a security measure. It stated that the route is based on security considerations. The committee did not see fit to interfere on military decisions. Azmi Bishara is being prevented from running in the forthcoming Israeli elections.

'The only security will be justice,' said Ghassan. 'If they end the occupation, there will be justice and peace.'

17. An Israeli–Palestinian Venture

23 January 2003

A few weeks ago, I answered an email request for an Arabic-speaker to accompany a Palestinian woman with breast cancer from a West Bank town to Hadassah hospital in West Jerusalem. The woman

Jerusalem: Old City in foreground

– let's call her Anna – had had a mastectomy last September. Anna is in her mid-sixties but looked a lot older. Infections had spread and, four months later, she now had complications which meant she could not complete the treatment for cancer, including chemotherapy. An Israeli organisation called Physicians for Human Rights (PHR) became aware of her case and arranged for her to be seen in a West Jerusalem hospital.

A special permit was needed for Anna to enter Israel a few kilometres from the town in which she lived. Usually West Bank Palestinians – even if they are sick – have to appear in person at the office of the Israeli Civil Administration for their area to obtain a permit. Somehow PHR managed to arrange for me to collect it in Anna's absence. So, one Saturday, I drove in the pouring rain along settlement roads which skirt the town, with no Palestinian cars in sight. I took the wrong turning near a settlement. An Orthodox Jew waiting at a bus stop opened the car door and very kindly asked to see if he could help me, but we didn't share any of the same languages.

By the time I arrived at the office, which was 16km away from Anna's town, up in some hills far from the main road, I was in fog. There was not a soul in sight except an Orthodox priest waiting mysteriously in his car. I couldn't imagine how Anna, sick, unable to travel comfortably or to drive, would have been expected to undertake this journey. I was made to wait outside in the pouring rain, while two young Israeli soldiers checked to see if I had an appointment with Azhar (the person with whom PHR had been liaising, and to whom they had faxed their letter in order to request a permit). After five minutes, I was let through an automatic security gate, and into their tiny office. One soldier had broken English and the other talked directly to me in Hebrew even though I told him I couldn't understand. Another five minute wait. I had a feeling I wasn't being taken seriously so I called PHR and they called Azhar directly. Then one of the soldiers went out apparently to find him.

Meanwhile, the first soldier asked what I was doing here. In the course of our conversation, he described how he wasn't allowed to be nice, even to the smallest Palestinian boys, because they weren't trustworthy. And the same story came out that I'd heard many times before. Ehud Barak (the former Israeli prime minister) had offered the 'Arabs' everything at Camp David. He had asked them, 'What do you want?' and then given it to them. And they refused and responded with violence. The other soldier returned and handed me Anna's permit to enter Israel. So I never got to meet Azhar – but grateful, I drove back.

When the day of the hospital appointment came, Anna's town was under curfew. I found a driver who said he would take us, despite the curfew, and we went to get her. She was waiting in the street with her husband and son, both of whom have mental disabilities. Her other child, Silvia, was in prison inside Israel for stealing a car a few years ago. So there is no income in the family and Anna cannot afford medical treatment. It was through their prison work that PHR had been in contact with Silvia and knew about her mother's difficult circumstances.

The taxi driver drove through the empty streets, and dropped us off out of sight of the soldiers. Together Anna and I walked slowly through the silent checkpoint. No one appeared, nor stopped us, nor looked at the permit. As prearranged by PHR, on the other side an Israeli woman called Nora came to meet us in her car and together we drove to the hospital.

It always amazes me when coming into Jerusalem from West Bank towns where Israelis are not allowed to go, that here, in the celestial city, Israelis and Palestinians can still walk some of the same streets, and rub shoulders with each other, even though they rarely share the same transport, let alone live in the same districts.

Hospitals, however, provide another place where Palestinians mingle – or even lie side by side – with Israelis. We found our way through a maze of corridors to the oncology department. Nora went into action in Hebrew with the rather hostile administrative staff to arrange payments, and I explained to Anna what was happening. She was a bit dazed. Because of an administrative error, we missed an appointment with the doctor we should have seen and had to wait several hours for another one. The waiting room was full of Jewish Israelis – many from Russia – and some Palestinians. The nurse we saw was a large Russian lady whose Hebrew was not very strong. Together Nora and I pieced together Anna's case history for the nurse . . . with a lot of questions and a few of the papers Anna had with her from medical appointments in her town. It seemed a bit precarious and didn't seem right that Anna's personal medical history was left in our amateur hands.

The oncologist was polite, but spoke no Arabic. I helped undress and dress Anna and told Nora in English what Anna was describing in Arabic. Nora then translated into Hebrew for the doctor. The wound from the operation had not healed properly. It turned out that really Anna needed to see a surgeon . . . so we were sent on our way to Emergencies.

That might have been the end of my involvement with the family but a few weeks later, Silvia called from prison to find out how her Mum was, and told me she was due to be released early due to good behaviour. At the same time, I was alerted by a Russian Israeli woman who spoke almost no English, Hebrew or Arabic, but who had made a prison visit, that Silvia's life was in danger.

She told me to call other friends (actually Christian Israelis – or 'Messianic Jews') who had visited Silvia in prison, and I found there was a story circulating that she was a suspected collaborator.

Palestinian society today is full of collaborators, many of them young men who have been arbitrarily arrested and detained by the Israeli army, and then are persuaded to collaborate. There is little mercy for such people. Collaborators, when found, are shot dead by firing squad. Silvia began to fear that this would be her fate too.

I got caught up in a week of phone calls between PHR, lawyers, social workers, friends, all of whom were trying to ascertain whether or not there was a real death sentence on Silvia. My first contact with Jewish settlers in the West Bank was actually when I was referred to an Israeli couple living in a large settlement, who were part of another Messianic Jewish ministry. They had found out, from Palestinians they were ministering to, that Silvia had been denounced as a collaborator within the Palestinian Authority.

A complicated set of possibilities emerged: Silvia had certainly got herself a bad name. She'd been involved with a gang of men when she stole the car. They were implicated in drugs deals and illicit sex. It seemed there were deep problems within her extended family, possibly involving property. It could have been that other members of her family, who felt she was bringing them all into disrepute, had spun the collaborator story, or it might have been the Palestinian Authority, or the criminals with whom she had been involved. Though we had assurances from the family that they would not harm her, we had to assume she was in danger. Prisoners have been shot at checkpoints on their release. Two girls from the same district had been shot dead a year before; why they were killed remained a mystery. We began looking for an alternative place for Silvia to stay.

On the day of her release it seemed the Israeli Civil Administration found out about the collaborator story. PHR tried to get her a permit to remain within Israel, out of danger, but they were refused. Silvia was handed over to the Israeli army and driven to the checkpoint nearest her home town. Nora and I met her and I passed on to her a mobile phone so that we could contact her. We saw her handed over to a local nun, who offered her a refuge until a Palestinian social worker could try to ascertain what the real dangers were.

That day Anna went back into hospital in her own town. Silvia took the risk and went to see her and ended up staying the night in the hospital, rather than with the nun. She was overjoyed to be reunited with her parents for the first time in two years. When I visited a few days ago, Anna looked happy too.

Anna remains unwell, but Silvia is alive. She has now decided, whatever the risk, to stay back at home in her parents' house. She tells me their house is black with damp inside, and so cold that it has made her mother's illness worse. The family are supposed to receive help from the social welfare office of the Palestinian Authority but there is no money there either. Silvia is determined to live a better life. She prays that no revenge for her old life is imminent and she hopes that the circulating rumour of collaboration will be forgotten. She remains in touch with her Israeli friends and is still hoping that PHR might be able to help her mother further.

18. A Bridge Too Far

Sunday 18 May 2003

Just before a quarter past six this morning I heard a loud explosion. It was someone blowing himself to pieces. The howls of sirens sounded straight away as ambulances sped towards the scene of the blast. This was the second Palestinian suicide attack of the morning, but this time only the bomber was killed: challenged by Israeli soldiers as he approached a checkpoint, he refused to stop and blew himself up. Earlier, a nineteen-year-old Hamas supporter disguised himself as an Orthodox Jew, got onto a bus, and detonated a bomb he'd hidden under his white prayer shawl.

List of martyrs' names on a wall in Gaza

Seven passengers died with him, and flowers are now being laid beneath the concrete flyover where the explosion happened.

Last night, the chief Palestinian negotiator, Saeb Erekat, resigned. In his parting speech, he said he didn't want to be led on another dance by Sharon in the talks around the 'Road Map'* to peace. The Road Map was to be implemented rather than discussed, with both sides taking the required steps in parallel rather than sequentially – i.e. Israel to freeze settlement activity in the West Bank and Palestinians to end violence. He also reminded us that since the Road Map was published on 30 April, dozens of Palestinians have been killed.

The road so far has indeed been rough. The day after the Road Map's publication and the formation of a new Palestinian government, Israeli tanks backed by helicopters raided an area of Gaza City after midnight and laid siege to the house of the family

---

* The 'Road Map' for Middle East peace was designed by representatives of the United States, United Nations, European Union and Russia in September 2002.

of a Hamas militant. Soldiers called on family members inside to leave the house, but they refused, witnesses said. Among the seven Palestinians killed in the gunfight was Amer Ayad, a two-year-old struck by a bullet to the head, and a thirteen-year-old boy. Fifteen others were wounded. On 14 May, three policemen and a child were killed in Gaza. The next day a further three Palestinians were killed in Beit Hanoun, northern Gaza, including Muhammad Zaanen, a twelve-year-old Palestinian boy who was shot in the head and left to bleed for three hours because Israeli troops prevented paramedics from reaching the scene. After some negotiations, he was eventually transported away by an ambulance but died on the way to the hospital. Muhammad joins the statistics of 370 Palestinian and 92 Israeli minors who have been killed since September 2000.

Tom Hurndall, a twenty-one-year-old British volunteer with the International Solidarity Movement (ISM), was shot in Rafah, south Gaza, two weeks ago:

> . . . he saw machine-gun fire being directed at a mound of earth on which about twenty children were playing. Most of the children fled but three young children were too scared to move, two girls and a boy aged between five and eight. Tom walked forward and picked up the little boy, named Salem Baroum. Having brought Salem back to safety he returned for the second child. Tom was shot in the head by a single sniper bullet as he leant forward to pick up the little girl.
>
> The Israeli Defence Force [i.e. the Israeli army] released reports that Tom was armed, clothed in army camouflage and firing at the soldiers. They have also released a report saying he was involved in crossfire. These reports have been reflected in media around the world, especially in Israel. These reports are not true. Many of you will have seen photographs of Tom in his fluorescent orange activist's vest. We have photographs of Tom immediately before and after the shooting – from several independent sources. There were over ten eye-witness reports of Tom's shooting – including the accounts of journalists – all of which support the fact that Tom was fired at with no justification.

But what is extraordinary is that to this day, not a single one of these witnesses has been questioned by the IDF or the Israeli authorities.

[Extracted from a recently published speech by Sophie Hurndall, Tom's sister, available on websites including www.squall.co.uk and www.countercurrents.org. An Israeli soldier of Bedouin origin has since been charged.]

Shortly after Tom and the British cameraman James Miller were shot in Gaza (Tom is in a coma, and James was killed), the Israeli army made all internationals, including United Nations staff and most diplomats, sign a disclaimer in order to enter Gaza. The statement declared that it is not the fault of the army if the person signing is shot. But since last Sunday – less than twenty-four hours after the departure of US Secretary of State Colin Powell from Gaza – the Strip has been totally closed to all internationals, including the UN agencies. Those inside cannot get out, and no one and no supplies can get in. The world must not see what is happening there. Furthermore, the offices of ISM near Bethlehem have been raided, and many peace activists deported.

Entering densely populated areas and using heavy weaponry to crush militants and all who surround them is not conducive to a peace process.

This morning's suicide bombings have yet again provided a perfect pretext for Prime Minister Ariel Sharon to delay his trip to the USA to meet President Bush to talk about the Road Map.

The bridge under which the bomber detonated himself and others this morning is the new road which has been built as the filter road into the Jewish settlements in East Jerusalem. It runs roughly parallel to the main road connecting all the Palestinian suburbs – Shufaat, Beit Hanina, then Al Ram and Ramallah. No Jewish settler living in Pisgat Ze'ev (where one victim of the bombing lived) need ever pass through the 'Arab neighbourhoods'. In fact, even the report in *Haaretz* (the *Guardian* of Israeli media) today erroneously referred to the bomb blast as taking place in the 'northern Jerusalem neighbourhood of Pisgat Ze'ev . . . close to the Green Line*.' The line between what is a 'settlement' and what is a legitimate Jewish 'neighbourhood' is increasingly being blurred in the Israeli public's eye. Pisgat Ze'ev is the wrong side of the Green Line to be legitimate. Arab East Jerusalem now houses two hundred thousand Jewish settlers – more than the number of Palestinian residents. The land the settlements are built on was confiscated from twenty-eight West Bank Palestinian villages in 1967. A network of roads and bridges connects the settlements, and has placed a stranglehold on the remaining Palestinian areas. I am wondering which roads will have to be dismantled for the Road Map to be successful?

19. Holes in the Map

3 August 2003

In May, the Masadeh family house was demolished. Last week (29 July) the Municipality of Jerusalem demolished the home of the El-Salfiti family in Silwan, East Jerusalem. The home provided shelter for twenty-two people. This week, the Ministry of the Interior has issued dozens more demolition orders for houses in East Jerusalem. This is in spite of the explicit prohibition of house demolitions in the short text of the Road Map: 'The Government of Israel takes no actions undermining trust, including demolition of Palestinian homes as a punitive measure or to facilitate Israeli construction.'

---

*'Green Line': after the cessation of hostilities between the Arab countries and Israel in 1948, an armistice agreement was signed in 1949. The agreement delineated the borders of each party and designated the 'no man's land' between them according to the location of their respective armies. This line demarcated the borders between Israel and the West Bank and Gaza Strip as recognised by the international community. It is worth mentioning here that Israel does not specify the boundaries of its state. Although the line became known later as the 'Green Line', its proper name is the '1949 Armistice Line'. Source: Joint Project notes by Applied Research Institute in Jerusalem (ARIJ) and the Land Research Centre (LRC).

The home of Sufian Masadeh (thirty-two), his wife Sana (thirty) and their children ranging from ages five to twelve was demolished even though Sufian had a letter from the Jerusalem Municipality stating that his house is in an area zoned for building and he was in the process of obtaining a permit. Mr Masadeh, formerly a driver, has been unemployed for the last one and a half years. The administrative order to demolish the Masadeh family home was originally given despite water, telephone and *arnona* (municipal tax) records dating back more than the thirty days before the first visit by a municipal inspector (all of which should make it impossible to obtain an administrative order). The court decided that the Masadeh family might have begun paying these bills before moving in.

There are two reasons the Israeli government uses to explain the continuing house demolitions, despite the Road Map: one is that the Road Map doesn't cover East Jerusalem because it has been formally annexed to Israel (it is 'occupied territory' under international law); the second is that the demolitions do not count as 'punitive measures' because they are being carried out for planning purposes. In the area where I live, 'planning' seems to mean the building of settler-only bypass roads through Palestinian areas, helping to connect the Jewish settlements by a road grid.

Impending demolition of the Masadeh house

The demolitions are part of a demographic war to bolster the number of Jewish settlers in East Jerusalem (currently two hundred thousand) and to reduce the number of Palestinians in 'Arab' neighbourhoods. A solid Jewish block in East Jerusalem makes the division of the city into two capitals (East Jerusalem for a Palestinian state and West Jerusalem for Israel) virtually impossible.

Last week I sat in an East Jerusalem shop, having my shoes mended. 'What do you think of the Road Map?' I asked.

'They are laughing at us. There will be peace for six months, then it will all be over,' the men replied cynically. 'The Israelis don't want peace.' I asked them what they thought should happen in order for there to be peace. The reply was clear and direct:

'Release Palestinian prisoners from Israeli jails; give back the whole of East Jerusalem to the Palestinians as their capital; and acknowledge and address the Palestinian refugees' right to return home.'

As we talked a string of greetings drifted through the door.

'You see this woman?' they said.

I looked and saw an old woman in traditional Palestinian dress bending down to take a basket of things off her head, and then sit on their doorstep.

The house being demolished (photo © Jos Koster)

'Her house and land in Jerusalem were taken from her in 1948,' I was told. 'She comes here from her refugee camp in Ramallah, to beg and sell what she can to pay her electricity bills and buy medicine. Is this justice?'

I asked them how many of the five million Palestinian refugees outside the Occupied Territories they estimated would return if given the chance. 'More than half to Haifa, Tel Aviv, Jaffa . . . ' came the reply.

Although the Israeli army retreated in full view of the world's cameras to the outskirts of Bethlehem last month, the town is, in fact, completely under siege. All roads around Bethlehem, Beit Jala and Beit Sahur remain blocked or manned by checkpoints. The number of people able to reach their jobs, families, hospitals or universities outside the town remains unchanged. In addition, the new 'security fence' is driving a wedge between Bethlehem and Jerusalem and taking with it vast tracts of Palestinian land on which Jewish settlements have been built.

The only difference is that Palestinian police now operate in the city itself. They, rather than Israelis, now stop cars and fine drivers without insurance and licences. Most people have not been able to obtain or afford these in the last three years because of the closures. 'We are still under siege,' my friends there said the other week. 'The "liberation" was just for the international media.'

20. Monitoring Violations

26 August 2003

Little has changed on the map of life for ordinary Palestinians since the Road Map was set up. At the end of July 2003 the majority of the two million Palestinians in the West Bank were surrounded by a hundred and thirty-three permanent Israeli-controlled military checkpoints plus – in the north alone – twenty-nine iron gates, two hundred and twenty-two earth mounds, fifty-two roadblocks plus twenty-two thousand metres of ditches and trenches sealing off roads and tracks around villages and towns. In addition, 'flying' or mobile checkpoints are erected daily. In fact, when a permanent checkpoint like Surda is ceremoniously dismantled as a concessionary step, a few days later three flying checkpoints have replaced it, and therefore it is now operational again, just as before. So much for progress under the Road Map.

The horrific scale and cruel nature of the Jerusalem suicide bombing on 19 August may lead many people to think that it was Hamas who was the first to violate the ceasefire. The images of injured and bloodstained Jewish Orthodox worshippers pierced many hearts, especially when it was revealed that among the twenty people killed were three-year-old Tehilla Nathenson, eleven-month-old Samuel Zargari, nine-year-old Yissaschar Dov Reinitz and three-month-old Samuel Taubenfeld. However, the bombing was Hamas's revenge for Israel's targeted assassination of several of its leaders in the preceding weeks, which they regarded as a gross violation of the ceasefire agreement.

The sequence of events was thus: on 8 August, the Israeli army entered a Palestinian refugee camp in the West Bank city of Nablus and killed two Palestinians. On 12 August, Palestinians killed two Israelis in separate attacks – one in Ariel settlement in the centre of the West Bank, and the other at the entrance to a shopping centre. On the night of 13–14 August, Israel invaded Jenin and Qalqiliya to make arrests and imposed a curfew in Hebron before surrounding the house of a wanted Palestinian, Muhammad Ayub Sider. Israeli troops fired heavy weapons at the house for three and a half hours. By dawn, it was completely demolished, and Muhammad Sider was dead.

Meanwhile, those Israelis who can't afford cars, or don't drive, live with the fear of boarding a bus. Isobel is a Jewish widow in her sixties from Chile. Every week she takes the bus into Jerusalem to our Hebrew class. Her children speak Spanish, Hebrew, Arabic, Polish and English between them, yet she has survived mostly on Spanish for ten years. She used to live in Baqa, a middle-class suburb of West Jerusalem, but moved a year ago to Har Homa, one of the most visible and controversial settlements, built on land belonging to Bethlehem (described earlier, in report 4, 'Bethlehem Views'). Why did she 'overstep the line' into occupied territory? Because, for her, the only line was financial and the monthly rent in Har Homa is US $350 cheaper than in West Jerusalem. When I asked her about the separation barrier that now runs below the settlement next to Bethlehem, she shrugged. I'm not sure she comprehends the political implications of settlements. I doubt if she even thinks of herself as a 'settler'.

Others in my Hebrew class do. Moshe is a Texan who has recently brought his family of five young children to live in Shilo, a settlement in the heart of the West Bank. He was a Christian who converted to Judaism on a close reading of the Old Testament, and he firmly believes the land belongs to the Jews. He seems a mild-mannered character who simply wants to live according to 'biblical principles'. I asked him if he had a gun yet, but he said, 'You have to be here for three years first.' Excavations in Shilo reveal an ancient Jewish place of worship and, for Moshe, they confirm his destiny here. This was, after all, where the tabernacle was erected, where Hannah prayed for a son and where Samuel was born. Moshe is unaware of the roadblocks, checkpoints and earth mounds because he doesn't have to see them when he drives to and from Jerusalem on roads that are exclusively for Israelis.

The ceasefire, which had significantly reduced fatalities and injuries, finally broke when Israel assassinated Ismail Abu Shanab in his car in Gaza City on 21 August. He was one of the most moderate Hamas leaders, and was in fact instrumental in persuading Hamas to agree to the ceasefire in the first place. A father of six, with five grandchildren, he had been born in a Gaza refugee camp, educated in the USA, and became a Hamas activist during a ten-year period in Israeli jails. He was the Palestinian prime minister's main liaison with Hamas, yet Israel held him responsible for orchestrating the Jerusalem bus bomb. A hundred thousand Palestinians poured into the street to escort his body in the funeral procession.

The ceasefire is no more and everyone I have spoken to here – Israeli or Palestinian – is convinced that there's a lot more bloodshed to come. A poll by the Israeli Dahaf Institute published in the Israeli daily *Yediot Akhronot* on 13 June found that two-thirds of Israelis want a halt to Israel's practice of 'targeted killings' of Palestinian activists. Targeting moderates like Abu Shanab undermines the fragile position of Abu Mazen and it does not ensure the security of Israeli citizens.

21. Tales from a Hornets' Nest

29 September 2003

There is an Arabic proverb which says: 'The one who counts the beatings is not the same as the one being beaten.'

The longer I stay here the more I realise I am the one watching the beating. However much I empathise with the suffering, I remain free and able to walk away at any time and am not enmeshed in the same confusion of lies and emotional turmoil that a conflict brings. International presence here is always welcomed, but some Palestinians remark – quite rightly – that it has not brought their suffering to an end.

A few days ago I was in the Old City of Nablus, the biblical city of Shechem, an ancient Palestinian town with labyrinths of secret alleyways and timeworn stone stairways leading round corners to houses. Like the Old City in Jerusalem, this Old City has come to house the poorest people, and those with money have long since moved to homes outside the old walls.

Since Nablus is also believed to be a hive of 'terrorists', or 'Palestinian militants', its residents are regularly terrorised by the Israeli army, who make raids day and night into the city. A few days before I sat in their crumbling stone house, Inas and Majdi and their children experienced one such raid which has left their lives in peril. At two in the morning they heard noises and found that Israeli soldiers with tracker dogs had surrounded their house and

View of Nablus

were on their roof. Then they beamed a laser-torchlight inside. Inas tried to tell them that her children were sleeping. To no avail. So she took the children into the street and went to her neighbours.

Next there was a loud noise and everything trembled. 'I thought it was an earthquake,' said Inas. She came back to find that the Israeli army had blown up two of her rooms – the kitchen and a bedroom. A fridge with its door hanging off could still be seen amongst other furnishings. The explosion also destroyed part of a neighbour's house below theirs.

Rania, their two-year-old daughter, said that the soldiers who killed Fadi – a local young 'martyr' from Nablus whose poster is locally prominent – 'killed her fridge', too. When asked why they had done this, the army, who brought their own journalists to document the action, claimed the house was a bolthole for Palestinian resistance fighters and a cache for their explosives. That's the first Inas knew of it. Apparently the house was once a jewellery shop. Maybe some remnants of jewels were thought to be explosives? Whatever the reason, the family are now all sleeping and living in one room and the walls of their house are so seriously cracked that the local Palestinian Municipality has said the property is unsafe and advises the family to leave (but offers no material help). Inas is the breadwinner in her family because her husband (who said nothing while I was there) is asthmatic and has heart problems. She works as a cook for old people. Elegantly dressed in black, attractive, unveiled and young, she asked me, 'Where do we go to? Everyone comes and photographs us. But nobody helps.'

Tales abound of Palestinian men (often the young ones) living in Nablus being beaten up as a result of mistaken identities or unproved allegations. I met a woman with a sick, unemployable husband and twelve children. One night, her son was shot in his left elbow in the alleyway outside his house. He'd heard a voice calling him to stand still, but he thought his friends were teasing him. Israeli soldiers beat him up, shot him and had him imprisoned for four months, probably because his brother was already in an Israeli jail. Though just eighteen, he is now the family breadwinner. Kindly-looking, his left arm pinned up underneath his T-shirt, he's in a lot of pain, but can't afford any drugs. The operation he needs to put his arm right can't be done in the West Bank. On the same night he was attacked, the army had entered his family's home by blowing a hole in the end wall. Much of the interior facing had been ripped away, and what's left of the house is now damp. The family have survived economically because people help them. Asked about their future, the young man's mother says: 'It will be worse than what has gone before . . . but al Hamdu Lillah (praise be to God) in spite of all the misery we still have to smile.'

Protection for civilians, as enshrined in international law, is a very rare commodity in this conflict. An eighty-two-year-old man was another unfortunate victim in the hornets' nest. Hearing shooting in the street below a few weeks ago, he came to his window to see what was going on. He died instantly in a hail of bullets through his chest. He has now joined much younger folk on the posters of the martyrs around the city.

For all the assassinations of armed Palestinians and trainers of potential suicide bombers, Israel is also committing many, many untargeted and indiscriminate acts of violence under the guise of self-defence, which only serve to create more terror, fear and resentment among innocent civilians. Some Israelis are courageously refusing to cement Israel's occupation of Palestinian land further, such as the twenty-seven Israeli air force pilots who this week refused to fly aggressive missions against civilian targets in the Occupied Territories.

A friend of mine recently heard two old men talking. One said: 'The situation between Palestinians and Israelis reminds me of a man holding a bee in his hands. The bee wants to get free and stings the man's hand, while the man keeps holding the bee because he thinks that by doing so he protects the rest of himself. An imprisoned bee will always sting. The man could either crush the bee between his hands or open them to let the bee go free. The first choice is called "genocide", the second is a courageous act opening the way to peace. The solution is in the man's hands.'

22. The Writing on the Wall

1 November 2003

Today as I came through the main checkpoint into Bethlehem – newly reinforced with concrete barriers for the start of Ramadan – two old ladies were pushing a supermarket trolley towards the taxi I was heading for. Dressed in traditional embroidered robes, and undaunted by the complaints of the driver, who wanted a quick getaway with me for a higher price, they started to unload sack after heavy sack and heave them up onto his roof rack. They had not carted these olives past the young Russian-speaking Israeli soldiers who were staffing the checkpoint, but had come round it on a mud track to the side, having been picking them in some nearby olive grove since six o'clock this morning. They could not have slipped their produce round the other side of the checkpoint as it has recently been swathed in two-metre-high rounds of new shiny silver barbed wire, the trade mark of 'the Wall', which now comes right up to Bethlehem. It surrounds the nearby fortress of Har Homa, as well as Rachel's Tomb, inside Bethlehem, enabling bus loads of Israeli tourists to continue to visit the shrine. Would-be local Christian and Muslim pilgrims to the shrine, meanwhile, remain trapped in the city as they have been for three years,

People passing through a gap in the wall, Abu Dis (photo © Jos Koster)

unable to make such a pilgrimage there or to leave Bethlehem. Gaps in the security apparatus remain, however, through which people over the age of fifty-four (and, theoretically, under the age of one), can still risk travelling to make a trade. These wrinkled business women, smiling through their metal-capped teeth, told me they could sell a kilo of olives in Bethlehem market for the equivalent of about £1.

It was by slipping through a gate in a completed section of the barrier near Jenin that Hanadi Jaradat, an attractive twenty-nine-year-old Palestinian lawyer, was able to blow up herself and nineteen other people at a restaurant in Haifa on 4 October. Every suicide bombing increases the support of the average Israeli citizen for the barrier because they associate it with increased security. Hanadi's murderous act appears to stem from having seen her brother and cousin killed in Jenin during an Israeli army operation there in June. When people want revenge, it seems they will find a way, barrier or no barrier.

On 23 October, the Israeli Ministry of Defence published, for the first time, a map outlining the route of the 'separation barrier', which it is building inside the West Bank to stop Palestinians entering Israel. So far about a hundred and eighty kilometres have been constructed. When complete, it will run for over six hundred kilometres – excluding the Jordan Valley side. The barrier is not monolithic: it is in fact different things at different points. But much of it is a fence, fitted with motion detectors and electronic sensors, surrounded on both sides by deep trenches, military patrol roads and swathes of barbed wire. Like this it spans between 60 to 100 metres. In other parts it is an 8 metres high concrete wall punctuated by armed concrete lookout towers. It penetrates deep inside the West Bank, winding around many Jewish settlements, and thus keeps them on the Israeli side of the new border.

The land between the barrier and the Green Line looks set to trap around two hundred thousand Palestinians inside what Israel calls a 'seam zone' or 'closed zone'. New regulations issued on 2 October require all Palestinian residents already in this zone to apply for permits to continue to live in their houses, farm their land and travel. The permits issued so far have been found to be valid for periods of between four and six months only. Yet Israelis of Jewish descent are permitted freely to settle and work in this area. According to the Negotiations Support Unit of the Palestinian National Authority, the order 'effectively grants any Jew in the world the right to travel freely throughout the Closed Zone while denying the same rights to the Christians and Muslims who live on, farm and own the land.' And all this inside the Palestinian West Bank, which according to international law is illegally occupied. Another case of new Israeli laws which masquerade as necessary and logical regulations to bring about security and order, but which actually annex more land, blur the fact of occupation, and continue to impoverish the lives of ordinary people. As I write, life for the Palestinian farmers and residents of the closed zone is grinding to a halt. Many of these people now join those who are dependent on food aid, because they're unable to farm their land, travel to work or earn an income.

Two Jewish settlers whom I recently met defy the widespread belief that all settlers are in favour of the barrier. 'I would feel safer if it doesn't come ... the community will stay more alert without it. It's a band-aid, a waste of money,' said one who lives in Shilo, in the heart of the West Bank. Another resident who believes that without a settler presence in the West Bank 'Zionism has no soul', expressed similar sentiments: 'The barrier is a psychological security blanket. It is useless.' It is currently estimated to be costing over £1 million per kilometre; at the same time many welfare benefits are being cut in Israel.

Last Thursday, a new section was announced for North Jerusalem. It will stretch from Qalandiya, the large checkpoint between Jerusalem and Ramallah, encircle the large Jewish settlements of Pisgat Ze'ev and Neve Ya'akov (near where I live in East Jerusalem), and enclose all the Palestinian suburbs and villages between it and the Green Line. Unless stopped, forty-five kilometres are due to be completed in East Jerusalem by early 2004. Already, fifty thousand people are divided from schools, shops, medical services and families. It has become a spectator sport for internationals like me, in the early morning hours, to watch children and adults climb over concrete blocks in unfinished sections or, if small enough, squeeze through gaps to get to school and work. Two colleagues of mine currently drive a loop of twenty kilometres on settlement roads to avoid climbing over the wall when it is only a distance of five kilometres from their homes to the office.

The barrier is the final death knell for the two-state solution. In the 1947 UN partition of the land, the Palestinians were offered forty-five per cent of Mandate Palestine. After the war of 1948, when Israel was created, the Palestinians were left with twenty-two per cent (the West Bank and Gaza). In the war of 1967 Israel occupied the twenty-two per cent. The Oslo Accords (1993) enshrined a process by which Israel would hand back the twenty-two per cent. Seven years of negotiations produced little tangible result and saw the number of Jewish settlers in the Occupied Territories double. In its current projection, including the not-as-yet-unveiled plan for the Jordan Valley, the separation barrier will leave two Palestinian enclaves on about half of the twenty-two per cent – that is, approximately ten per cent of what was originally Mandate Palestine. The oft-quoted rhetoric of a 'viable Palestinian State' will effectively become two seemingly non-viable ghettos in the West Bank plus the prison which is Gaza, already surrounded by a fence. Three and a half million people are currently being rounded up. This is the writing on the wall.

Publisher's note
Because of the frequently changing situation with approved and built sections of the barrier, it could be misleading to include a map here. Readers are referred to the websites on p.8 for current information.

23. The Fear of Separation

7 December 2003

The plane lands at three forty in the morning, at Tel Aviv's Ben Gurion airport. A female security guard stops me on the tarmac before I can get on a bus to the terminal and asks for my passport. What do you do in Israel? What is your job? Who do you know? More questions rattle. She furiously presses buttons on her hand-held information device without looking at me. Becoming more aggressive in her tone, she reels off even quicker demands for information, and appears frustrated by whatever data she's getting back from her device. The last people off the plane file past us and fill up the bus, leaving me alone with her. I turn my back to the bus, imagining many suspicious eyes trained on me. A few minutes later, still pressing buttons with her eyes averted, she finally gives up, promptly hands back my passport and says I can go. I step on the bus and it moves off to the terminal. Welcome to Israel.

Now I stand in the 'foreign passport' queue. My lane is slow. After ten minutes I approach the window, and a diminutive but cross-looking young official greets me: 'Morning. Where do you live?'

'Jerusalem,' I answer.

'Yes, but where?' she says impatiently.

I tell her the name of the neighbourhood in East Jerusalem where I live.

'Well, why didn't you write it down?'

'Because I don't have a street address,' I said truthfully, having written down my PO Box number.

She fumes. 'You know the procedure.'

'Do you mean the Ministry of the Interior office?' I ask. It is now a quarter past four. She nods.

'Will you bring my passport?' She nods again. So I stand alone a few metres away, next to the MoI office, watching everyone else go by. As usual young security guards mill around holding foreign passports and having earnest conversations with their seemingly idle peers, as if they are dealing with a subject from Guantanamo Bay. Fifteen minutes later, the same girl slowly saunters up with my passport and slaps it on the table, and leaves. The ministry official (another female) carries on a telephone conversation in loud Hebrew. It finishes. Nothing happens. She gets another call. I lean on the door post and wonder, should I intervene, or would that slow things down still further. Finally, I say, in the next pause between calls, 'That's my passport.' She looks at me, then at the passport, as if she hadn't seen it, types my details into her computer, updates her records in some way, and hands back the passport with a gate pass.

So now I approach the gate. A young man takes my passport and starts the normal questioning procedure. I make the mistake of telling him I have already been questioned. The first round is predictable: Why do I work here? Why was I in Jordan? (from a previous visa) Do I know anyone there? How long have I been here? Who pays my salary? What is my job? He goes away to consult a superior (female). He comes back for a second round.

'But why the Middle East?'

'Because I'm interested in the development side of this conflict,' I say vaguely, trying to think of a way to avoid showing my interest in Arabic and all things Middle Eastern.

'Do you know people here?'

'Yes.'

'Who?'

'Israelis and Palestinians.'

'What names?'

'Do you mean the names of our partner organisations?'

'What is the connection between your work and helping people here?' (I ask for clarification on that one.) It's half past four. He goes away again for more consultation, as if in training.

Somehow the end is predictable: I have to have my luggage re-x-rayed. I walk to the other end of the hall and queue. Am now in the hands of another security guard. Fortunately, only one other unfortunate foreigner is in front of me. A kind guard hands me a tray for my duty-free bags. It all passes through. My passport is still withheld. 'Follow me,' says someone else. I follow her to a small room which she opens with a code. I step in and the door closes. I walk back and forwards through an electronic sensor. I beep. My shoes come off and are scanned separately. Then it's all over. My passport is handed back – 'Have a nice day' – and I'm free. My taxi driver is still waiting for me, over an hour since landing time, and I drive to Jerusalem. We drive on the Modi'in Road, a new Israeli-built road, a convenient short-cut from Jerusalem to Tel Aviv, making the drive to the airport significantly quicker. It goes illegally through the West Bank, and in places slices Palestinian areas in two. On the way, in the murky dawn light, I see an Israeli police van blocking a Palestinian car on the other side of the road. A Palestinian is being questioned, away from his vehicle. He looks vulnerable and unprotected and after my short but intimidating airport ordeal, I shudder at what Palestinians routinely face when trying to move about on their own land.

This week, the Israeli newspaper *Haaretz* printed a map showing how 'the Wall' is coming to North Jerusalem. The wall will come down the centre of a main street in a busy commercial district. More than sixty thousand people who live on the east side of it will become West Bank residents by default and lose their Jerusalem identity cards. Nobody bothered to tell these residents

Pisgat Ze'ev settlement, East Jerusalem; with a Palestinian home in the foreground

that this would happen. Some found out when they spotted an Israeli surveyor in the street. One newspaper put it aptly – 'barring a miraculous last-minute change, a wall will soon go up in the centre of their main road, a wall that will separate students from their schools, storekeepers from their stores, patients from their doctors, lovers from their loves.' Ironically, the World Bank is one of many organisations which will be trapped on the east side. Needless to say, the wall encompasses the large Jewish settlements of Neve Ya'akov and Pisgat Ze'ev near here, ensuring they stay on the western (Israeli) side.

The fear of separation is not just experienced by Palestinians in the West Bank. The annual public opinion survey of the Jaffee Center for Strategic Studies in Tel Aviv University, published in late November, finds that one-third of Israelis support the expulsion of the Palestinian citizens of Israel from Israel. This is the highest percentage ever recorded in the survey. Israeli Housing Minister Efi Eitam, of the National Religious Party, said recently, 'The Arabs in the country are creating a situation of chaos from the perspective of rule of law.' These areas in which there is a Palestinian majority (more than a million Palestinians live in Israel, as Israeli citizens) worry Eitam. 'In another ten years we will not have effective sovereignty in Galilee and in the Negev, but rather only a formal one . . . My main task as housing and construction minister is to strengthen the Negev and Galilee with Jewish settlement.'

He has been true to his word. At the end of October, the Israeli government announced the construction of more than three hundred new homes in Jewish settlements in the Occupied Territories: a hundred and forty-three new apartments in the Karnei Shomron settlement in the north of the West Bank, and another hundred and eighty in Givat Ze'ev, north of Jerusalem. Meanwhile, the 'Road Map', of course, requires Israel to freeze construction of all settlements in the West Bank and Gaza.

As I write (7 December 2003), two workmen have just turned up at my house with my landlord. They left their homes in Nablus this morning at five. It is now half past midday. They have come to do a small repair job in my house, re-laying some tiles. The man has just shown me the bottom of his trouser leg, which was covered in mud. They had to walk and travel by donkey half way across a mountain to get out of Nablus. As soon as I asked him whether he had a permit or not, he said angrily, 'No. You have to tell America, this is what it is like for us. They just don't know.' Desperate for work, he, like thousands of others, had risked his life by circumventing the checkpoint, to come to Jerusalem for this job, unable to obtain a permit to leave Nablus 'legally'. If Palestinians were donkeys, the whole world would be in uproar at their treatment: something often said by Palestinians themselves.

24. Quiet Before the Storm

18 January 2004

As fast as the preparations are going and the paranoia growing, amongst both Israelis and Palestinians, as they ready themselves for a showdown in the International Court of Justice in the Hague in February, the separation barrier is going up.

Lawyers for the Israeli side are readying their case about 'military necessity', while eight-metre-high concrete sections of wall are being laid this week through the heart of East Jerusalem. No longer can old and young squeeze between the cracks, climb over temporary concrete blocks or circumvent hastily laid barbed wire to get to their hospitals, schools, doctors or workplaces. This time, the separation barrier has come for real, in new and final looking form, even though the Israeli government stands by its statement that it is 'temporary'. Meanwhile Palestinian suicide bombers continue to strike at Israeli interests, blowing apart many lives, not least their own. This week's explosion at the Erez crossing into Gaza distinguished itself in that the perpetrator, a woman called Reem, aged twenty-one, was a mother of two. Reports say she was urged on by her husband to join the ranks of the martyrs. Those she killed were youngsters like herself, aged nineteen, twenty, and twenty-two.

Opponents of the barrier have been pushed further into the spotlight with the shooting of Israeli demonstrator Gil Na'amati two weeks ago. Shocking his parents, this non-anarchical Israeli, who grew up in a kibbutz in the western Negev, joined a group of protesters for the first time. Less than two minutes after cutting into the barbed wire he was shot in the leg, and almost died from loss of blood. The Israeli media are now bristling with barrier reportage.

It seems shortsighted to place so much faith in the barrier to stop attacks. Three things militate against its horizontal efficiency: Palestinian Qassam rocket technology, based in Gaza, which is growing apace; tunnels, which have been used extensively in history to defeat borders such as the boundary between Egypt

An Israeli demonstration against 8m-high slabs being laid in East Jerusalem

and Gaza; and the enormous destruction and misery being sown on one side of the barrier, which is unlikely to generate peaceful feelings towards those living on the other.

A farmer I spoke to in Qalqiliya was philosophical. He lost his land behind the separation barrier over six months ago . . . and wondered why anyone was bothering to protest any more. 'This land was colonised by the Greeks, the Romans, the Ottomans and now the Israelis. But it belongs to God.'

The mayor of Barta'a – a town of four and a half thousand Palestinians on the Green Line that has been completely ringed by the barrier, with just two gates in it – described to me last week how they had fought with the Israeli military over the permit system just imposed on them. Everyone living in this enclave had to accept a permit to remain a resident there. Lying on the 'seam-zone', this town profited from textile factories. In addition to young local women, six hundred girls from all over the West Bank were coming to work there until the barrier went up. Now they cannot enter through the Israeli-controlled gates into the enclave without permits. They have applied, but have not yet got any. Some stay in the enclave 'illegally', sleeping either in the factory or in rented rooms at night.

The barrier changes not only the social culture of the town, but local diet. The enclave population now goes for weeks at a time without tomatoes or cucumbers or eggs from the West Bank. It seems to depend on the mood of Israeli soldiers whether produce is allowed to enter through the gate or turned away. Waiting at the gate this week, I saw small boys dragging enormous sacks of provisions as well as carrying their school books. That day, they were allowed to pass on foot, after inspection and questioning in the pouring rain.

It is widely agreed by observers from all angles that this barrier is about more than security. Annexing large swathes of prime agricultural land, demolishing houses in its way, creating enclaves and necessitating a new identity and permit system to control the movement of ordinary people, the barrier is certainly brutalising the West Bank population. However, the argument that it is about terrorism can be persuasive. Israel has now hired a French PR company, Publicis, to help them form a media relations strategy to deal with international public opinion around the Hague judgement on the barrier's future. Publicis, apparently the largest PR company in Europe and fourth largest in the world, has advised Israel to change the name from 'security separation barrier' to 'the barrier for the prevention of terror' – yet another link in the convenient 'war on terror' rhetoric.

In the so-called 'period of calm', or 'eighty-one days of quiet' between terrorist attacks against Israelis, a steady stream of Palestinian militants and civilian bystanders were killed by Israeli forces, from Rafah in Gaza to Jenin in the north of the West Bank. Then daily raids into Nablus from 15 December turned into full invasion and occupation of this major West Bank city on 26 December, one day after a suicide attack north of Tel Aviv. In the largest offensive since April 2002, hundreds of soldiers, dozens of military vehicles, tanks and bulldozers poured into the city and stayed there for twelve days until the Feast of the Epiphany (6 January). The city and Balata refugee camp were put under curfew while soldiers hunted for and killed militants, bystanders and children (including a five-year-old in the refugee camp). Houses were knocked down, had windows blown out or holes knocked through them, rendering them unfit for human habitation. A total of thirty-eight families were affected, according to the UN report. While the local population were trapped in their homes, troops destroyed several buildings of great architectural and historical value in the heart of the Old City. There were many recorded incidents of soldiers preventing medical teams from reaching the wounded. At least fourteen Palestinians died and fifty were injured during the whole period.

Amjad al Masri, a fifteen-year-old, was one of those killed on 3 January, as he watched others throwing stones at Israeli soldiers from his rooftop. According to his father he was just watching, when he was hit directly by live fire and died. His eighteen-year-old cousin Muhammad was near Amjad's body in the funeral a few hours later when he was also killed by a shot to the head (in disputed circumstances). Amjad's sixteen-year-old brother Iyad was traumatised, and reportedly bent on revenge. By the next day he had become a suicide bomber, but was apprehended and blew only himself up. Iyad had not previously belonged to any militant group. In an interview with the *New York Times* from his home in Nablus, Iyad's father directed his sharpest criticism at fellow Palestinians who turned Iyad into a human bomb. 'Those who sent him were not supposed to do that,' said Masri, who is forty-four. 'They were supposed to understand his situation and not to let him do such a thing, even if he asked them.' The condemnation of those who recruit bombers was also echoed by Dr al Masri, a distant relative and member of the Palestinian legislature. 'This was a great mistake, and the one who made this mistake should be made accountable' (Greg Myre, *New York Times,* 14 January 2004). The military necessity of this particular raid created at least one suicide bomber. Many of the others who have decided to give up their lives and shatter those of the 'enemy' have also lost relatives in similar raids.

Walking through the silent Shabbat streets of West Jerusalem, passing the occasional Orthodox Jew in black hat and suit, I felt a lifetime away from the noise on the other side of the barrier. Eating lunch today (18 January) in a European-style restaurant amongst many Israeli families, and discussing whether anti-Semitism is on the increase with my non-Orthodox Israeli friend, I wondered which will be more persuasive to the judges in the Hague: military necessity or humanitarian catastrophe?

On 9 July 2004 the International Court of Justice in the Hague ruled that Israel's separation barrier is illegal by standards of international law and recommended its demolition. The court also said the route of the barrier is not vital to Israel's security and that compensation must be paid to those Palestinians whose property was confiscated as a result of the construction.

25. Divide and Rule

Part One

17 March 2004

Driving through East Jerusalem at school-leaving time: tiny uniformed Palestinian children shot across the main road like rabbits. As I turned right at the French Hill junction, where Jew meets Arab, and went down the hill, the people became bearded and Orthodox with black hats, the cars became different models, and the houses changed from disparate shapes to the identical units of the settlement blocks. Half an hour later, down into Israel proper, I was in a former kibbutz, among pine trees and bird-filled springtime hills. As I was singing some Mozart with my teacher, who came here from New Zealand some forty years ago, Gaza City was being bombed by Israeli air forces, in direct retaliation for a suicide bombing at the Israeli port of Ashdod two days before, in which ten Israeli workers died. This, the first attack by two Gazans, was a wake-up call to Israelis who believed that the fence around the Gaza Strip (ringing off the settlements from the Palestinian areas), together with a tight border control, could prevent suicide bombers infiltrating Israel. In addition the attack was jointly owned by the Qassam Brigades – the military wing of Hamas – and the Al Aqsa Martyrs Brigades, an offshoot of Arafat's Fatah party. The bombing was carried out to revenge savage attacks by the Israeli army on two West Bank refugee camps.

Tonight we are expecting a full onslaught in Gaza. Israel has declared it will continue to target leaders of militant groups, in spite of the high civilian fatalities in these assassinations, because the Palestinian National Authority will not take any action. The PNA, however, is an organisation in tatters, incapacitated largely by Israeli military onslaught, rife with rivalries and dogged by corruption. Still at its head and imprisoned in his Ramallah compound is Yasser Arafat, who appears immovable and unable to exert any influence over the militant groups. Not surprising really, given that, according to some historians, in its beginning as the Palestinian movement of political Islam in the Occupied Territories, Hamas was supported by Israel as a rival to the dominance of the PLO's national movement.* 'Hamas', which is Arabic acronym for the Islamic Resistance Movement and also means 'zeal' in Arabic, is not only a political movement fighting for an end to Israel's occupation of Palestinian land (and for some

---

*Ilan Pappe argues that the Israeli government's Orientalist advisors recommended that it solidify political Islam as a countermove against the national politics preached by the Palestinian Liberation Organisation but that when political Islamic forces turned against Israel with more force than the PLO it was too late. See Israeli historian Ilan Pappe's *A History of Modern Palestine – One Land, Two Peoples,* Cambridge University Press, 2004, p.249, and Palestinian historian Ziyad Abu Amr, *Islamic Fundamentalism in the West Bank and Gaza,* Indiana University Press, 1994, pp.5–19.

ideologues, an end to Israel), but it is also part of a network of Islamic welfare institutions. Hamas soup kitchens feed the poor, try to re-house those whose homes have been demolished, and run a vast social welfare system. Attracted by this focus and cohesion, a number of Fatah party leaders in Gaza who are disenchanted with their colleagues in the West Bank have reportedly joined Hamas in recent weeks. At the same time, rivalry for control has manifested itself in the murder of several prominent Fatah members by masked gunmen.

The fragmentation in Palestinian society is tangible locally too. This week for the first time a Palestinian bus driver outside the Old City of Jerusalem asked me not only to produce my passport but insisted on seeing that my visa was valid before allowing me on the bus. Getting stopped by Israeli police between Jerusalem and Bethlehem, carrying 'illegal' passengers – which is to say, those without the required permit to be in this area – could put him in jail.

My friends in Deheishe refugee camp in Bethlehem – living on the corner of a narrow alleyway, between damp, dirty walls, sparsely furnished with mattresses for sleeping – were squabbling. The father, unemployed for the last four years, remains visibly depressed and irritable. The mother, who is ill, defends her seven-year-old daughter when she is hit by an older brother. In this cooped-up existence, which is all the children have ever known, she wonders where she can get the treatment she needs, and worries about how to pay for the extra tuition for her seventeen-year-old boy, the brightest of her children, who wants to study medicine. I see no reason why the pressure within Palestinian society should not boil over. It seems likely to lead to expressions of anger towards westerners in general, who do not seem to be changing the situation of Palestinian society, but have become a standard part of the occupation, relieving Israel of its humanitarian duties towards the occupied population. The Occupied Territories crawl with UN and international charity vehicles, but nothing ever appears to change. We are propping up a deteriorating society.

Katharine's fiancé Felix beside a section of the wall in Bethlehem

Part Two

24 March 2004

'Yesterday was the worst act we've done in years,' an Israeli Knesset member said to me, 'It turns it from a territorial to religious conflict. This prime minister is more dangerous to Israel than he is to the Arab world. We will find ourselves in a religious conflict which is not solvable.' The assassination of Sheikh Ahmad Yassin, founder and spiritual leader of Hamas, is predicted by many around the world to escalate the conflict seriously. Firing a missile at a wheelchair-bound man leaving a mosque in a quiet Gaza street at dawn – even if he was an inspiration for acts of murder – presents a chilling image. As chilling as a blast on a bus which shatters unknowing human beings into fragments within seconds. Almost forgotten in the furore of Yassin's assassination are the deaths of the seven other civilians, including a young boy, who were sacrificed to achieve Israel's military objective. That objective, according to many Israelis and Palestinians here, was to enrage the Palestinian nation, increase intra-Palestinian rivalry and fuel further hatred and violence towards Israel. And, were these seven civilians any less innocent than the ten Israeli workers killed in Ashdod on 17 March? In this part of the world, innocence is subjective.

Today I sat in the Israeli army court martial of Yonatan ben Artzi, aged twenty-one. Yonatan started conscientiously objecting when he was sixteen, the age that all Israeli school children begin to receive letters from the army, beckoning them towards compulsory military service. Better known than some pacifists because he is the nephew of Benyamin Netanyahu (former Prime Minister, current finance minister), Yonatan was told that he was not, in fact, a pacifist, but only thought that he was. He was convicted of refusing to obey orders to enlist in the Israeli army, and 'withdrawn from the army' because he was 'not sufficiently motivated'. He spent nineteen months in military prison and detention centres. Today's final courtroom scene was a surprisingly shoddy procedure, with ill-disciplined exchanges between the high-pitched young army prosecutor and an army judge, flanked by two army officers. Unfortunately an interview Yonatan had given to the Israeli newspaper *Haaretz* last week was used as evidence of his 'egoistic' character in wanting to pursue his university career and refuse national service. There is no framework within the government or military for dealing with pacifists, or with the growing number of young Israelis who do not believe in Israel's need to defend itself inside the Occupied Territories or in the means it uses to do so.

Meanwhile, identities are easily confused. Three days before the murder of Yassin, a twenty-one-year-old man was jogging through the largely (but not exclusively) Jewish settlement at French Hill in East Jerusalem when he was shot dead in a random drive-by attack by Al Aqsa Martyrs Brigade who mistook him for a Jew. Actually, he was a Palestinian Christian, from a prominent family whose father is a well-known lawyer in Israel. His funeral in a church on the Mount of Olives drew unprecedented numbers of mourners, including one friend of mine who studied chemistry with him at school. Simple but false divides: Jew, Arab, Christian, Muslim, innocent and guilty. It seems that a terrible polarisation is occurring, not only here but globally. It is a dangerous by-product of the 'war on terror'. Western – especially American – military tactics around the world, and particularly in Iraq, give support, tacit or explicit, to many of Israel's military actions against the Palestinians. The Knesset member I spoke to said that because targeted assassinations are seen as an acceptable means of 'fighting terror' by the United States, this gives 'international permission to do things which are unbearable'. The US's lack of condemnation of Yassin's death was much noticed but tragically expected here.

The week before he was killed, Yassin and other political leaders of Hamas were engaging in constructive talks with Islamic Jihad leaders and the Palestinian Authority about how to share power and control Gaza in the event of the much-publicised Israeli plan to withdraw 'unilaterally' from the Strip. 'Once this occupation is over, it will be our right to participate in the authority which administers this land,' he had said. All hopes of Palestinian co-operation, and endeavours to halt the disintegration of Palestinian society in the face of the occupation, were shattered when that missile hit the wheelchair.

26. Independence Day

27 April 2004

The celebration of Israel's fifty-six years of independence ended tonight at sunset. Blue and white national flags were draped over cars, buildings and houses, and attached to lamp posts throughout Jerusalem, and fireworks exploded into the night. Since its miraculous establishment, Israel has safeguarded the rights of the Jewish people and given them a haven from the ravages of anti-Semitism. The rights of many others in the same land, however, have been eroded. While the world has been glued to the spectacle of Israel's high-profile assassinations of Palestinian militants and their leaders in recent weeks, the sophisticated machinery of the occupation continues to destroy life in more subtle ways. Living in caves and rough hillside dwellings for the last two hundred years, the residents of the south Hebron hills have been subject to a sustained attempt to evict them and destroy their unique way of life. These peasant farmers, who lost much of their agricultural lands behind the Green Line when Israel was created in 1948, recently had their crops sprayed from the air with poison and their caves filled in with rubble by Israeli bulldozers. Overlooked by three illegal outposts, Jewish settlers use violent means to prevent them from farming their land and passing up the valley to get to Yatta, the main Palestinian town in the region, on which they depend for food and trade.

Farmer's sons harvesting

Last Saturday, however, the farmers knew they were not alone. Together with busloads of Palestinian and Jewish Israelis from the Israeli organisation Ta'ayush, I arrived in their fields. We had come to help them clean out the caves that were filled in, and assist in harvesting their crops. Twenty of us climbed into the back of a white truck and drove seven kilometres east, through wide fertile valleys, on a twisting mud track that was sometimes not mud, but just rock. Hearing our worried shouts in the back as the van tilted dangerously and scraped over stones, Ahmad, the driver, mercifully decided to take ten of us at a time for the second half of the journey. Arriving at a village, just below Suseya settlement, we pulled up barley stalks (and occasionally thorns by mistake) for goat feed. 'They come with guns and threaten us, and cause us all kinds of misery,' said the farmer's wife, referring to the settlers. Her family have lived there for three generations in spite of the odds.

Declared a 'firing zone' after the Israeli occupation of the West Bank in 1967, and then a 'military drilling zone' in the 1980s, their land has been snatched from them and their houses destroyed.

The farmer's wife

However, they continued to dig out caves – a skill developed over the last two centuries – and live in them. Then came the illegal Jewish settlements of Ma'on, Karmel, Suseya and Beit Yatir, also in the 1980s, built in a strategic line across the southern edge of the West Bank. Since then repeated attempts have been made to evict these communities, using military orders, court procedures and the establishment of outposts, whose fanatical inhabitants are disliked by the more conventional settlers. The co-operation between the Israeli government, army and settlers seems to be tight. During Ehud Barak's government, bulldozers and trucks came and destroyed cave dwellings and water wells and hundreds of people were expelled. Last September, two tanks came and obliterated their fields and crops. And at four o'clock one morning four jeep-loads of settlers accompanied by the army came and evicted residents from their caves. The absolute death knell for these communities will be the separation barrier, which is going to loop round the settlements to keep them territorially contiguous with Israel. In doing so the barrier will include those who live south of the settlements, cutting them off from the rest of the West Bank. It will sever farming communities completely from their services and food sources in Yatta. They, like others before them, will have to apply for permits every six to twelve months to continue living on their land. The only rationale for Israel's brutal behaviour appears to be a desire to force these communities to migrate, freeing up more land to expand Israeli territory. That is what the separation barrier seems to be doing wherever it has been built.

And the rationale for the route of the barrier, rather than security, is the settlements, now sanctioned officially for the first time ever by an American President. Settlements in occupied territory, which are prohibited by international law, seem to have won the day. The construction of the separation barrier has already strangled Bethlehem on all sides, and is now going south, fast approaching the Hebron area in the south of the West Bank. With few water wells, and no access to other villages, it is hard to see how these peasant communities will survive once the barrier is built. Dotted along the last hills of the West Bank before the descent into Israel, these communities feel isolated and remote. It is difficult to believe that just a few kilometres away sits Israel, a sophisticated and wealthy country which they saw rise on their land less than sixty years ago.

Hillside cave-village of Jinba

Postscript

Since I wrote the above, *Haaretz* reported (4 May 2004) that the Civil Administration has destroyed eleven structures including 'shacks, tents and public facilities erected by the British government's Department for International Development'. What the paper described as 'large forces of IDF [Israeli army] troops and border policemen, accompanied by bulldozers' came to demolish them – this was despite the fact that Palestinians and Civil Administration are still awaiting mediation following the evictions of 1999 in the area, and the High Court of Justice ruling in 2000 that the residents had the right to return.

27. Beyond the 'Gateway of Terror'

12 June 2004

Two days ago during the night, bulldozers moved into the street round the corner from where I live in East Jerusalem and ripped up one side of the tarmac road. In a simple move, they'd cut the artery between Jerusalem and Ramallah, 19km to the north. The artery will bleed for a few days, while the people of this area in between – Al Ram – still try to move between the two, by walking several kilometres from one checkpoint to another, until the separation barrier is finally up. Then there will be no more movement on this stretch. Only huge grey slabs of concrete down the centre of the main street, defining the people on one side as Jerusalemite, and on the other as West Bank. It's now a common sight to see a single slab being transported through the city, needing a whole lorry to carry it.

The encroaching wall, with its further increase in restrictions on movement, is on everyone's mind. A few hours back, in a shop in the Old City of Jerusalem, two well-dressed middle-class Palestinian

Al Ram: Muslim Friday prayers, held as a protest in the street where the wall is to be built

The wall coming down the middle of the road, Al Ram

ladies came in and swiftly chose some beautiful ceramics as presents for their relatives in the USA. They interrupted our conversation with the store's owner, to plead with him to deal with their purchase quickly. 'We only have a permit for one hour before we have to be back at the checkpoint to Ramallah,' they said. Eloquently, the store owner lamented his own dilemma: the oven where he fires all the ceramics is in Al Ram, on the wrong side of the street. He doesn't know what to do. He may have to close his shop, in a prime location in the Christian quarter of the Old City, and sell the business – if he can. In the half hour I was there, the shop attracted international, Israeli and Palestinian customers.

It just takes one close look to realise that the separation barrier is not simply about security. Seeing the silent, bearded security guard, with his cap on and a gun round his neck, standing next to his jeep by the new section of wall which has been built right into the town of Bethlehem, I recently felt like I was in some wild-west movie. Israel has simply staked its claim on the land. It's difficult to see the barrier as anything other than a land grab. Otherwise it could have been built in a different place – i.e. along the Green Line.

Israeli jeep at Al Ram checkpoint

Rumours have circulated for the last year about which route the barrier will actually follow in Al Ram. Different maps have been published in the local press and thousands of left-wing Israelis have demonstrated here in the last few weeks. After months of speculation, the community's fears are now being realised. On Friday, the local Muslim community held its prayers on top of the newly torn-up road as a form of protest. The prayers were fervent and heartfelt. Afterwards, they walked up to the checkpoint. Young boys picked up rocks in anger. Israeli soldiers and jeeps calmly stood in wait behind the barbed wire. Some Palestinians urged the crowd back. Others burned tyres in protest. I left before anyone was hurt.

So many people were hurt last month, I couldn't bring myself to write. In May 2004, one hundred and eleven Palestinians were killed, the majority of whom were unarmed civilians. This is the largest number of fatalities in a single month since the Intifada started nearly four years ago. As Israel swept its tanks and helicopters over Rafah, in the southern Gaza Strip, over two thousand

Israeli tank at Sufa Terminal near Rafah

people lost their homes. Local hospitals were overflowing with dead and injured, and bodies had to be placed in food freezers, because ambulances could not get through the chaos and checkpoints to pick up the dead. And the Israeli army found another tunnel, through which arms are apparently smuggled from Egypt. The international community condemned the incursion as a war crime, but nothing stopped it except, perhaps, media coverage of Israelis firing tank-shells on hundreds of mostly unarmed Palestinians who were demonstrating against the loss of their homes. Then they felt the heat, and withdrew for a few days. For the first time, I, like many others working here, was paralysed by a terrible feeling of impotence. Rafah was described by Israeli General Ya'alon as the 'gateway of terror' yet behind that we witnessed a terror being inflicted and the creation of a humanitarian disaster. Millions of dollars are needed to repair the damage caused to the area by Israel, but it will be, as usual, the international community which pays.

During the time that internationals were not permitted to enter, all I could do was go to one of the entrances of the 'gateway of terror': the Sufa terminal, three kilometres from Rafah, near the border with Egypt. Again, it was like travelling to the moon. In a desert landscape, Israeli soldiers were quietly cleaning and maintaining their tanks. There was little noise and no sign of battle. No one took much notice of me, and everything seemed 'normal'. Walls and barriers to understanding are sadly everywhere. 'No, I've not been in there,' said one young female conscript, nodding towards the Gaza Strip, while innocently telling me which crossing I could use to try to get in. I could imagine tank drivers rolling into Rafah, never having met a Palestinian, and understanding nothing of Rafah residents' experience as second, third and fourth generation refugees. To bulldoze a house must take a strong mind, as must firing on unarmed civilians without even warning them with tear gas. While walls of concrete are going up, it will be difficult for anyone on either side of the 'gateway of terror' to understand or be concerned for the lives of anyone on the other.

28. From Grotto to Ghetto

6 September 2004

It seems appropriate to write the last of my reports from the place where they began – Bethlehem. It is nearly two years since I first arrived in October 2002. In that time, Bethlehem has been sealed almost entirely into what can only be described as a ghetto. I am writing this in my car, whilst waiting in a line of others to get out of the town through the main checkpoint. In a few weeks this will all be changed.

'Israel comes up to here now,' a teenage Israeli security official has just told me with a naïve grin, pointing down at the ground. Dwarfing him is the terrifying spectre of the eight-metre-high concrete wall that almost encloses the town. The building of the wall has moved Israel closer to Bethlehem by four hundred metres. The land south of the checkpoint that did belong to Bethlehem will now be on the 'Jerusalem side' of the wall or separation barrier,

Israeli security guard at the new entrance to Bethlehem

and as such will become part of municipal Jerusalem. A neat way to expand your borders.

Slouching next to the official on a chair in a makeshift tent is a private security guard with a massive gun round his neck. I walk deliberately close to them and take pictures of the gap in the wall which they guard, and which in three or four months, they tell me, will replace the well-established checkpoint for ever. The gate will be the only opening for Palestinian residents to pass in and out of their town. There will be a separate entrance for tourists, and a separate one for Israeli settlers and pilgrims wishing to visit the cave shrine of Rachel's Tomb inside Bethlehem town. An Israeli settlement has already begun around this shrine, so its Jewish future is ensured. 'Whoever has a permit, can enter Israel,' said the guard grinning again, referring to the Palestinians in Bethlehem who have little chance of obtaining permits. I thought of Venice in the Middle Ages, and how the Jews were locked up at night in an iron foundry, the origin, I believe, of the word 'ghetto'.

Prison walls require cunning from those who would breach them. A European-looking man bent down and looked at me through the window as he walked past my car. A few minutes later he returned and asked if he could hitch a lift with me into Jerusalem. After 15 minutes' wait and a show of my passport we sailed through the checkpoint. Posing as a German, the man, I discovered shortly afterwards, was actually Palestinian, a native of Bethlehem, who had learnt German from his friends and practised as a hairdresser. He had so far been able to get out through the checkpoint without a permit and go to Jerusalem to do things like fixing his laptop, because he looks European and keeps his hair long, which few Palestinian men do. Each time he comes back to Bethlehem, he enters via a different checkpoint. But his excuse on exit – that he has forgotten his passport, or left it in Jerusalem – is wearing thin.

I wonder who has the key to Bethlehem? The Israeli army? The international community? The Vatican, custodian of the holy Catholic shrines next to the Church of the Nativity? The Greek Orthodox who own so much of the land in Bethlehem now confiscated by Israel? The worldwide body of the Church? Is it really to Israel's benefit that Palestinians are locked up inside their towns?

That a democratic state has just built a wall illegally on the land it occupies, causing death and the incarceration of another people, defies all international laws. Yet so far, no one has been able to stop it. So the grotto of the Christ Child – the one who came to set us free – is in the centre of a town surrounded by walls, fences, barbed wire and a mesh of rules and regulations prohibiting the movement of over 60,000 people.

A few hours later I am sitting in the air-conditioned Café Hillel on Jaffa Street, West Jerusalem, watching the world go by and listening to soft latin jazz. All customers – it is now filled with middle-aged Israeli lady friends eating salads and drinking coffee – are loosely inspected by a very vulnerable (often Ethiopian) security man on the door with a metal detector. I know that even my more liberal left-wing Israeli friends feel safer sitting in this café because of the existence of the 'wall', as probably would I, living here on 'the other side'. A very pregnant woman walks in, and for a brief moment the thought flits through my mind that she could be disguising explosives. A silly, almost obscene thought. But a natural one here. Just a few days ago, I was trapped for 15 minutes in a shoe shop up the road, during a bomb scare which brought the army out to inspect some unidentified object a few metres away. It came to nothing. Such is life in Israel. Paranoia and fear understandably permeate it.

Two Palestinian suicide bombers struck two Israeli buses in Beersheva last week killing 16 Israeli civilians, the first such attack in nearly six months. What was hardly reported was that during this period of 'calm', over four hundred Palestinians were killed by the Israeli army in devastating heavy-handed incursions into Palestinian civilian areas. Less reported still, was that one of the bombers – a cousin of a friend of mine in Hebron, from a large and well-known family – had been singled out, harassed, pressurised and offered bribes by the Israel secret security for weeks prior to the bombing, to become a collaborator for them. He had refused. Ironically, the message to the Israeli people from this bombing was that the building of the barrier around Hebron needs to be speeded up.

What is happening in Bethlehem, and in many other towns, is happening to the Palestinian people as a whole. If you look at snapshots of the land which Palestinians own or live on, in 1948, 1967, 1993–2000 (Oslo) and 2004 (with the 'separation barrier'), a frightening picture emerges. The Palestinian population live on decreasing islands of land, no longer connected to anything that gives them life. As described throughout these reports, the systems of checkpoints, curfews, closures, ditches, earth mounds, the bypass roads connecting Israeli settlements and isolating Palestinian villages and towns, and the insidious and evil permit system, have strategically combined to render a two-state solution currently null and void. Palestinians live in what the most sceptical of people can only describe as ghettos, which are economically as well as morally unsustainable. Pockets of poverty close to poverty

Palestinians queueing to pass Huwarra checkpoint at Nablus in the midday sun

levels of sub-Saharan Africa are beginning to appear. Eighty per cent of Palestinians are under 30 years of age, so occupation is all they have ever known. Their options for the future seem to be growing narrower by the day, and they have little to lose.

It needn't be like this. I believe that money could go a long way to solve the crisis. Half the amount of American aid ($6 billion) given to Israel each year could persuade the majority of settlers to move back to Israel proper, through financial incentives. The fanatical ideologues, who have no sensibility of human rights beyond their own, are undoubtedly a future problem. But settlements with their monopoly on electricity and water could become the new homes for generations of Palestinian refugees who have only ever known life in a crowded camp. The wall, if moved to the Green Line, could become a recognised border between Israel and Palestine . . . and could be torn down in more peaceful times, when trust and economic and social relations have been rebuilt between two separate states. People and leaders need to start to dream of peace.

There have been several important and good pieces of news in recent weeks. The most significant was perhaps the decision of the Israeli Supreme Court to order the government to re-route thirty kilometres of the barrier and to take into account Palestinian rights in future decisions regarding the route. The second was the decision of the International Court of Justice in the Hague to judge the barrier to be illegal, reaching the right conclusion despite not the most robust of legal arguments, as I understand it. The third is the recent courageous decision of the three-million-member American Presbyterian Church to begin gathering data about its investments in private companies in order to support a selective divestment of their holdings in multinational corporations doing business in Israel/Palestine. These have given me hope.

Other developments are less positive and positively deceptive. The Gaza withdrawal if approved by the Israeli government this October, will grab the headlines as a 'breakthrough' for the next six months. If implemented as planned in February 2005, it would be the first time an Israeli government has ever released its grip from any of its settlements built in the Occupied Territories (a project of thirty years). Yet as part of this unilateral agreement comes the sealing in of the six main settlement blocks with their own roads in the West Bank which support and fix in place the Palestinian ghettos. And by the time the withdrawal is complete – which will not be without an immense and long drawn out fight from the ideological settlers – the West Bank barrier will be completed.

The Palestinian contractors I met near the wall in Bethlehem talked happily to the Israeli security guard, each speaking the other's language. 'Is this peace?' I asked them, pointing the camera. 'No,' they said, and waved the camera away. I asked the Palestinian workers, who were from Hebron, what they thought of the wall. 'We work on it, but we reject it,' they said, then were quick to explain that they didn't actually work 'on' the wall, but just prepare the ground around it. The security guard joked that they were actually collaborators . . .

Afterword

September 2004

I am very grateful to you, my readers, for encouraging me to write the emails and forwarding them on. They have been a vital outlet for me during my two years here and your feedback has kept me writing in the belief that it is worth recounting my experiences.

I may write again in a different series but for now the reports are finished, I am getting married and moving back to the UK.

I suppose I believe that change happens when people know the reality of the situation on the ground. This conflict tests that belief severely. I do think change will ultimately come and justice be done, but it may not be in my lifetime. However, I still have an instinct to help and I believe we must always try to witness to the truth.

Epilogue

May 2005

I arrived back into Israel's shiny new airport terminal aboard a flight packed with Jewish Orthodox families, many of whom had made the long flight from the USA. As the sun shone on the red-roofed houses near the coast, you could sense their happiness upon our safe touch down, and from their chat to their children, their sense of coming home. And I felt glad that Jews have a country in which they can feel safe.

In the eight months since I left, many developments have taken place that have caught the interest of the Western world: Yasser Arafat – the leader of the Palestinian people for decades, has died; democratic presidential and local government elections have been held – a model to many other Arab countries; a ceasefire has been holding tentatively between Palestinian militant groups and the Israeli army since February; there has been a marked decrease in the number of Palestinian militant attacks, and the Israeli government plan to withdraw its 7000 settlers from the

Gaza Strip has progressed it seems to the point of no return (due for implementation mid-August 2005). It sounds good, and many onlookers in the West are optimistic that now – again – there is the chance for peace.

Yet none of the Israelis and Palestinians I have spoken to on this trip have shared that optimism. They know that the reality on the ground in the Occupied Territories has improved little during this same period, and in many places has got worse.

The separation barrier has been creeping steadily through the West Bank, dividing Palestinian communities and cutting them off from all contact not only with Israel but from their very livelihoods in other towns of the West Bank; peaceful village demonstrations against the barrier have been brutally suppressed by the Israeli army resulting in some fatalities, and Palestinians living in the expanding seam zone, between the Green Line and the barrier surrounded by settlements, can only come and go from their homes through gates at restricted times controlled by the

A boy walks beside the wall at Abu Dis, East Jerusalem

army. While discussions are taking place about what to do with the settlers' houses and farms in Gaza after an Israeli withdrawal, thousands of new apartments are being built in the major settlements in the West Bank. While I was there Ariel Sharon announced publicly on TV that these settlement blocs, which are illegal under international law, would become part of Israel.

What can an Israeli withdrawal from Gaza mean if it also entails the completion of the barrier and the permanence of the Jewish settlements inside the West Bank? As long as both remain, the Palestinians will be subject to the checkpoints, gates and other means of control. A Palestinian state under these conditions is not viable.

'I will defend my people at any cost,' an Israeli security officer told me, as I questioned the brand new as yet unopened gate-and-checkpoint complex he was guarding next to the 8 metre high wall imprisoning Bethlehem. What will it take, I thought, for this young man to link the security of his own people to that of his Palestinian neighbours, whose land he now stood on?

Katharine von Schubert

The gateway to Bethlehem

Appendix

The Ecumenical Accompaniment Programme in Palestine and Israel (EAPPI)

In August 1949 the Fourth Geneva Convention, which Katharine mentions in 'Olive Picking' (report 5), turned international attention to the protection of civilians during times of war and under any occupation by a foreign power. The hideous punishments and reprisals exacted on innocent people by the Nazis and their allies were still vivid in the public mind. Just four months before, the last of the Nuremberg Trials had ended.

Article 33 of the Convention stated:

No protected person may be punished for an offence he or she has not personally committed. Collective penalties and likewise all measures of intimidation or of terrorism are prohibited.

Pillage is prohibited.

Reprisals against protected persons and their property are prohibited.

Given these unequivocal declarations, the logic of sending official observers, preferably from the United Nations, to Israel, the West Bank and the Gaza Strip would seem irreproachable. But, as Katharine notes in her 'Prologue', despite clear precedents in, for example, the former Yugoslavia and Rwanda, three attempts at the UN to establish a monitoring force were frustrated in late 2000 and during 2001. There then followed appeals from humanitarian groups in both Israel and Palestine, and a number of peace associations and the Churches, for human rights observers who could work independently of their governments.

Floresca Karanasou of Quaker Peace and Social Witness takes up the story:

In 2001 QPSW was discussing what new work to establish in Israel–Palestine, and in October that year the committee responsible for putting proposals forward to our Central Committee adopted a proposal to set up a one-year project to send human rights observers to Israel–Palestine. This idea made sense not only because of the calls coming from different quarters that there was a need for such work, but because QPSW already had substantial experience (and therefore the systems in place) for sending workers overseas, and to Israel–Palestine in particular. The proposal was approved by Central Committee in December 2001.

The QPSW observers project began in January 2002 and the first three observers arrived in Israel–Palestine in early June and returned in September. Another four followed in October 2002 and returned in February 2003. Katharine was part of this second team.

In January–February 2002 the World Council of Churches (WCC) organised a meeting in Geneva of all those churches from all over the world who were interested in implementing a human rights monitoring programme in Israel–Palestine along the lines of the WCC's Ecumenical Monitoring Programme in South Africa. They agreed a name, mission and objectives for what became the Ecumenical Accompaniment Programme in Palestine and Israel (EAPPI). Accompaniment here means protection by presence as well as solidarity with those Israelis and Palestinians who struggle nonviolently to end the occupation. The first WCC Ecumenical Accompaniers set off in September 2002.

During the same month various members of the Middle East Forum of Churches Together in Britain and Ireland, including the Church of Scotland, Christian Aid and QPSW, met in Edinburgh to discuss how churches and church-related organisations could implement the EAPPI. As QPSW was the only body there to have implemented a programme like this before, we agreed to be the implementing partner for the EAPPI in Britain and Ireland.

QPSW began the implementation of the EAPPI on behalf of a number of churches and church organisations in January

2003 and sent twelve Ecumenical Accompaniers that year. Since then it has been sending twelve each year..

In conclusion, here is part of the EAPPI mission statement:

The EAPPI is an international ecumenical programme with the mission to accompany Palestinians and Israelis in their non-violent actions and concerted advocacy efforts to end the Israeli occupation of the West Bank and Gaza Strip.

Participants in the programme monitor and report violations of human rights and international humanitarian law, accompany Palestinians and Israelis in acts of non-violent resistance, offer protection through non-violent presence, engage in public policy advocacy and, in general, stand in solidarity with the churches and all those struggling against the occupation non-violently. The programme is an initiative of the World Council of Churches, which responded to an appeal by the Heads of Churches in Jerusalem, who requested 'protection for all our people in order to assist the reestablishment of mutual trust and security for Israelis and Palestinians' and called on 'all peace-loving people from around the world to come and join us in a manifestation of just peace'.

The countries involved in the programme currently are Sweden, Norway, Switzerland, Denmark, Germany, South Africa, the United States, Canada, New Zealand, Finland, France, Britain and Ireland. From September 2002 till the end of May 2005 a hundred and ninety Ecumenical Accompaniers had served on the programme.

The EAPPI partners in Britain and Ireland with QPSW are the Baptist Union of Great Britain, the Catholic Agency For Overseas Development, Christian Aid, the Church of Scotland, Churches Together in Britain and Ireland and its Churches Commission on Mission, the Iona Community, the Methodist Church, Pax Christi UK, Trócaire and the United Reformed Church. Website: www.quaker.org.uk/eappi